RICHARD GILLETTE

the ART OF THE INTERIOR

RICHARD GILLETTE

RIZZOLI
NEW YORK

New York · Paris · London · Milan

CONTENTS

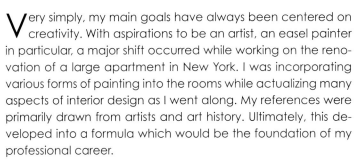

Very simply, my main goals have always been centered on creativity. With aspirations to be an artist, an easel painter in particular, a major shift occurred while working on the renovation of a large apartment in New York. I was incorporating various forms of painting into the rooms while actualizing many aspects of interior design as I went along. My references were primarily drawn from artists and art history. Ultimately, this developed into a formula which would be the foundation of my professional career.

When the opportunity presented itself to create a book on my work, the archive that had been building over time immediately flashed across my mind. The realities of devoting the time required—attaining original film images, deciding which projects to select, and countless other concerns—seemed insurmountable. Then came the realization that this was an assignment no more daunting than an extensive design project, something I'm very familiar with. Within weeks I agreed to go for it, and the parallels have been very similar indeed.

I want to thank my colleague Daniel Solomon for his consistent willingness to assist in every aspect of this multifaceted endeavor, from its design to its content. For this book we have gathered together 20 design projects from 1975 to 2008. We've been extremely fortunate to be able to use photographs taken by some of the most top-notch photographers in the business. Their gracious help has been invaluable. I also want to thank everyone for permission granted to run images of all of the paintings and sculptures that appear on the following pages.

The work that I sometimes refer to as mine is, in reality, the result of the contributions of so many people. There's a cavalcade of architects, contractors, artisans, craftspeople, and specialized dealers; imagine credits rolling with a continuous stream of names at the end of a movie.

Throughout this book, what I hoped to express was something about the remarkable people involved, where the action took place, and what occurred on each of the projects. This led me to put down bits of recollections for each apartment, house, and garden. The twist here is that along with my work, we have also included images of the art that the designs were born of. This has afforded me the chance to give credit to these artistic champions who I am continuously moved by, and trust that you will be too.

(Opposite) This photograph was taken in my TriBeCa artist's studio in the mid-1970s. By this time, my focus had shifted from stretched canvases to entire environments.

INTRODUCTION
by Wendy Moonan

The New York interior designer Richard Gillette is a bit of an enigma. He may be one of the most admired decorators in his profession but he is not well known personally.

While he has been featured in *The New York Times*, *Architectural Digest*, *Elle Décor*, and *House & Garden* today he does not maintain the meet-and-greet lifestyle of many of his colleagues. He doesn't run around town with an entourage. He doesn't appear at popular decorator-driven charity events. He keeps a low profile and is more likely to be spotted at the Metropolitan Museum than a furniture showroom.

An avid student of art history, Gillette says that as soon as he left upstate New York to attend college in Manhattan in the 1970s, "The Met became my home away from home." This is probably because, first and foremost, Richard Gillette is an artist. He trained at the School of Visual Arts in New York with such eminent instructors as Chuck Close and John Chamberlain and still does easel paintings for fun, wall murals for clients, album covers and backdrops for advertising and fashion shoots. "When I'm on a ladder all covered in paint I'm in heaven," he says.

His attraction to fine art has never waned.

"My references are primarily drawn from artists I admire and art history," says Gillette, who regularly visits museums and galleries. "Ultimately, this developed into a formula that would be the foundation of my professional career."

In the 20 short essays he has written for this book, he pairs each interior with a specific work of art that informed its style in some important way (such as palette, composition, or scale). The list includes Old Masters like Vermeer and Watteau, Orientalists like John Frederick Lewis, Surrealists like De Chirico, Cubists like Braque, and Abstract Expressionists like Rothko. The list is long.

Gillette follows no school of interior design; his spaces do not resemble English country houses, French chateaux, or Italian villas. Nor are they studies in minimalism. "A cookie-cutter signature style does not come naturally to me," he says. In fact, it is hard to identify a "Gillette look," though his interiors do tend to be theatrical. The look is decidedly eclectic.

"There is no period I don't love," he says. "Putting them together is what I do."

Every project is different because he takes his style cues from diverse sources: a client's dream, a particular work of art, a textile, a souvenir from a trip abroad—or a 1930s Hollywood film (especially those by Busby Berkeley). Most of his clients are creative types—movie stars, fashion designers, art dealers, and collectors—and some have employed him over decades for multiple projects, probably due to his highly personal approach.

For 15 years Gillette maintained a design office with partner Stephen Shadley, another successful artist-turned-decorator. "I think some collectors hired us thinking we, as artists, would know how to deal with their works of art, would know how to take our cues from their works and give them a cohesive unity," Gillette says. But they were all too successful. When the business got too big and the workload too stressful, Gillette took a sabbatical. Then, two decades ago, he established Richard Gillette Designs, a small shop with a hands-on philosophy.

Why? He likes to collaborate.

"It's never 'my way or the highway'; everyone I've worked with soon finds that there is a give-and-take with our relationship,'" he says. "I try to focus on who the client is and what the environment is longing for," he says. "We don't always agree at first. I tell clients, 'This is what you are looking for. This is what I am thinking. How can we come to a common ground?' "

He brings art reference materials with him to client meetings to illustrate his ideas. "Like any relationship, communication is the key to success." Notably, in the age of instant messaging, he insists on progressing slowly. "There is a common misconception that a project can be done in a matter of days, from concept to final reveal," he says. "My way of working can be challenging because it's so personal; the term 'organic process' sums it up the best." It is also time-consuming. He relishes commissioning custom cabinetry, upholstered pieces, window treatments and light fixtures. "This is not something you can do quickly," he says.

He employs a wide variety of artisans: bronze workers, carpenters, glassmakers, etcetera. "I like to break down the distinction between decorative art and fine art," he says. "And I like to keep craftsmen of every type busy."

His approach is well illustrated by a New York apartment he decorated for a Middle Eastern woman clothing executive who collects vintage textiles and costumes. In a vast loft (p. 162) he purposely carved out an intimate lounge by creating walls made from antique glass doors from Syria. Inspired by Leon Bakst's exotic 1910 set design for the ballet *Scheherazade*, he installed these doors with lacey Arabesques in carved wood, and then furnished the room with luxurious over-scaled green mohair banquettes and silvered low tables from India. He painted Moorish motifs and repetitive tile patterns that he had seen in Iran, Turkey, and Spain on a mural for the ceiling. Now it is covered with "faux tiles" in geometric patters of green, turquoise, orange, and black. "I took work from the Alhambra in Spain, mosques, and Topkapi Palace, so the ceiling would not resemble a given place," he says. The late Italian decorator Renzo Mongiardino would have loved it.

The *piece-de-resistance* is a mural covering the lounge's entire back wall. Gillette photographed his client's vintage embroidered black bolero jacket and had one small fragment enlarged 400%. He then papered the wall with the blow-up of the stitches, but now they look like rope. Finally, he proceeded to enhance the "stitches" by rubbing metallic powders on top to "give some glimmer and glamour and shimmer."

This is like couture decorating, Gillette says. "The piece was fitted specifically to the contours of the apartment. That's what true couture means."

Some of his interiors resemble stage sets, purposefully so. One way Gillette produces "theater" is through the use of a single, unexpected, bold stroke. One client, a Hollywood actress famous for her wit and quirky style, lived in a 1940s house in Sneden's Landing on the Hudson River north of Manhattan (p. 98). The house had a "great room" paneled in dark mahogany, even on the cathedral ceiling. Gillette bravely painted the entire space (ceiling, walls, and floor) in bright white, partly to show off the client's vintage Paul Frankl upholstered pieces. "We went to resources in a number of cities in search of chunky furniture to use as sculptural objects—as in a De Chirico landscape throwing off any consistent sense of scale," he says. Then came the genius moment. Gillette found and installed a pair of chandeliers, mid-century commercial fix-

tures, that were over four feet in circumference. Each had 140 porcupine-like spokes with lights at the tips. They hang from the ceiling "like star bursts" he says. The fixtures are the exclamation points in the stage set.

Another client bought the piano nobile in a magnificent 1918 Horace Trumbauer Beaux Arts townhouse in Carnegie Hill in Manhattan (p. 170). With its original walnut paneling and eighteen-foot ceilings, the living room resembled a Louis XVI salon in a French chateau, complete with gilt bronze sconces. But it was also charm free, more like a mens club. Enter Gillette, stage left. The client wanted to retain the wood walls and carved detailing, and Gillette agreed that the room's formality called for Neoclassical furniture. But how to make the place look like a twenty-first century project? Gillette designed a custom carpet 40 feet long and 24 feet wide with a Bauhaus grid and bright Leger colors: bright blue, green, yellow and an orange red, on gray. "I generated the design on a computer and had it woven in Nepal," he said. Then he painted the ceiling bright blue, added two contemporary hyper-realist contemporary paintings and, voila, he managed to eliminate the stiffness of the architecture. In the dining room next door, Gillette provided scenic murals since "the room has no views of its own." One wall depicts the dancing water fountains at the Chateau of Versailles. The wall opposite has an Italian landscape with tall cypresses, a bit like a painting by John Singer Sargent.

"This will be your garden," Gillette told the client. "These will be your views."

Ever inventive, he had found the images on line and had them scanned on to canvas panels scaled to the elevation of the vast dining room. The real fun came after the canvases were mounted, much like wallpaper, on the walls. "I painted over every surface for three weeks," he recalls. "The pixilated images looked too modern, so I covered them with translucent layers of paint and metallic powders—not to obliterate the pictures but to enhance them."

For the dining room's viewless window he designed lush full-length curtains "just like you would have on a stage," he says. Behind them, he replaced the glass in the French doors and put in a grid of colored, leaded glass in pale greens, yellows, and blues in what he calls a "Mondrian pattern."

"I had just been to Tahiti," he says. "My idea was, when the curtains were open, you would see water and sky. What the room is supposed to conjure up is romance—and put people in a cheerful mood."

Like professional set designers—and he has done a few theater sets—Gillette is obsessed with the manipulation of light. He often applies silver and gold leaf to ceilings and beams.

"How do you embellish something?" he asks rhetorically. "You use the techniques people have employed since ancient times: gilding and silvering."

Gillette is fascinated by anything that reflects light: the mother-of-pearl inlay in a chest from Damascus, mirrored furniture, lacquered anything. For translucent effects, he plays with shoji screens, curtains made of gossamer metallic fabrics, and hand-marbleized silk, and any number of iterations in glass: colored, frosted, leaded, rippled or patterned. He often suggests ebonizing floors for effect, "so the furniture appears to dance on the surface, like people on a Busby Berkeley set," he says.

For a traditional 1918 home in downtown Charleston, S.C. (p. 70), he produced a mélange of classical "influences," quite different from anything else he had done but appropriate for the setting. Furnishings included a Federal convex mirror, an alabaster and bronze Greco-Roman ceiling fixture, and window cornices boasting motifs taken from ancient Pompeian wall paintings. Floors are decorated with Adamesque painted medallions. He calls the house his "American Piranesi," after the eighteenth-century Italian architect who tutored Adam.

This kind of decorating, with such a vast range of references, cannot be duplicated, which is why this book is worth studying—and is long overdue.

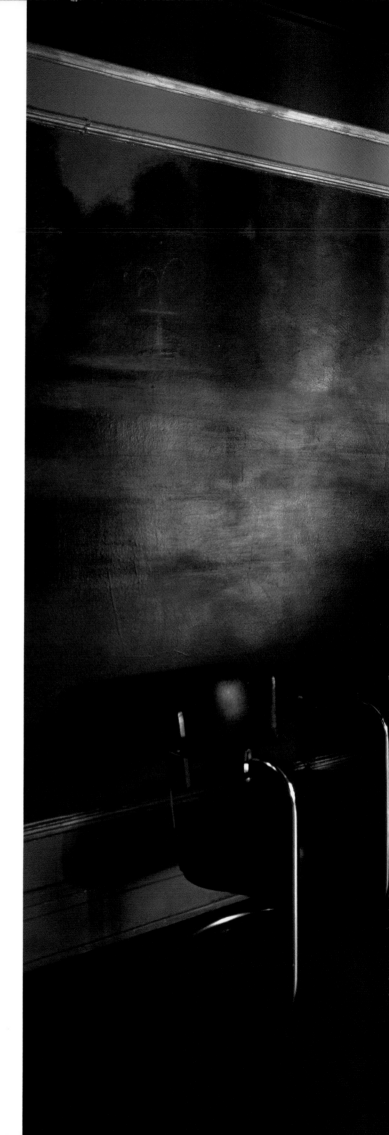

CUBIST ILLUSION
Upper East Side (Manhattan) - 1975

This apartment was the very first place where the concept of using rooms as paintings was realized. The building was from the 1940s, solidly built, but ordinary in style except for the support structure which was visible in each of the rooms. Square corner columns and ceiling beams, nice flat crown moldings, and narrow baseboards—in all, it had a modern boxy appeal. Although I initially resisted, I began to appreciate a newfound beauty in modernism.

While my brother, Francis Ricardo (a hair and makeup artist who was fast becoming a favorite of fashion magazines and ad agencies) was on location for one of his many sittings, I was in the new apartment painting the structural elements, studying the work of Georges Braque and Juan Gris (my favorites of the cubists), and asking myself how I could incorporate their use of severed flat cubes, wood graining, newspaper fragments, and chair caning. I already had the answer. Trompe l'eoil techniques were what I was using in the former apartment—fooling the eye, creating an illusion. Fortunately, one of my friends at the time was a well-respected painter and teacher at the Art Students League who saw where I was heading and rallied me on.

Shifting from canvases to wall paintings was labor intensive, but I was really having fun and had found a new approach. I transformed the support columns to look like wood with dark vertical grain to emphasize their height, the ceiling molding that surrounded the main room to light, horizontally striped exotic wood to play up its length, and split up the largest wall into large shapes, angled flat planes that read as distance—something I had seen in many of

Cezanne's paintings. My voracious appetite for making large pictures was satisfied.

The process required base coats and color, various painting techniques, dry brushing, rubbing with steel wool, followed by layers of varnish and then waxing and buffing. And finally, after weeks, the surfaces had the glamour of an environment that might have existed in the 1920s or 1930s. When my brother returned briefly between trips he was pleased and really understood that the apartment was becoming a large continuous work of art. A friend once said of us, "one brother makes up walls, the other paints faces."

The painted architecture continued from room to room including each door. There were twelve, each painted differently, all reminiscent of art deco cigarette cases. After discovering an illustrated book on Eurhythmics (a theory based on body movements and the patterns of musical notes), I began to do charcoal drawings on paper of these figurative images. The walls of the foyer and some of the main room were covered in twelve-foot-wide Belgian linen. It was then that the charcoal was used to produce the larger-than-life-size figures, evocative of the dancers in Matisse's lyrical painting, *Dance I*. Once the negative space was filled in with paint the walls took on a bas-relief appearance. With a fear of overworking the murals and obliterating the gorgeous linen fabric I stopped, considered them finished, and moved on to the empty walls in the bedroom.

We always made the analogy between Park Avenue and a canyon. Living there, especially with the rooms remaining almost empty, we really felt like we were hanging over a precipice. This was rather exhilarating. Our views were primarily stone and steel. Cubism—literally and virtually—and many pictures of the Grand Canyon from *Arizona Highways* magazines inspired the stylized images that covered the bedroom walls.

Spanning their entire length, these paintings, as well as the figurative murals, were lit by custom-built wall wash fixtures. Chrome-plated torch lamps lit the rest of the main rooms, lending a more specific 1930s period connotation. The look of the American-Modern Movement continued with an extraordinary triangle-shaped desk and a set of streamline furniture. The rest of the furnishings (sofas, cabinets, and tables) were all custom designs developed with my brother.

This experience was invaluable and helped me to realize that I did not have to choose whether to be an artist or a designer. It didn't have to be either/or. A cohesive blend of all of the arts and crafts traditions could be incorporated at once.

Ultimately other artists, architects, journalists, and people from the fashion world all made their way through the apartment. The assessment was unanimous that I should continue with this personal approach. The press picked up on it and offers followed. I hadn't found a profession, but a profession had found me.

(Opposite) Figurative murals on seamless Belgian linen begin in the entrance foyer and move through to the main area. Paint treatment poses as inlay exotic wood on the doors and doorframes. Action paint-splatter technique transforms the parquet floor.

(Above) ART REFERENCE: *Fruit Dish, Glass, and Lemon (Still Life with Newspaper)*, Juan Gris (1916). Cubism and Gris's palette of rich, deep hues were chosen for all the painted surfaces and furnishings throughout the apartment.

(Pages 16-17) In the lounging area, the exotic faux bois pillars (in Madagascar ebony) support the ceiling painted with architectural motifs. Two indigo satin custom chaise longues mirror each other. Eurhythmics, developed by the Swiss educator Dalcroze, taught music through movement. Wall murals illustrate his theory.

(Above) The longest wall in the apartment is severed into flat planes. Custom composition stone cast tables continue the cubist language. The windows are layered with rippled glass sliding (formerly shower) doors.

(Opposite Top) In the disconcerting service entrance, stalactite and stalagmite motifs are repeated in the mirrored wall. This is one of the twelve individually painted embellished steel doors.

(Opposite Bottom) ART REFERENCE: *Ultimo, An Imaginative Narration Of Life Under The Earth*, John Vassos (1930). This cherished book set the tone for the ambience of the environment. It's typical of its era, yet timeless.

(Pages 20-21) The Grand Canyon wall paintings parallel the Park Avenue canyon of stone. The triangular inlay American 1930s desk was discovered after completion of the bedroom. *Vogue* magazine (hair and makeup on cover by my brother) sits on top of a round table from the luxury liner, the *Caronia*. Custom wall wash lighting fixtures appear to be cantilevered beams.

(Top) In lieu of a bed is a set of American-Modern furniture. The abstract painting is by Peter Golfinopoulos (*Untitled*, 1976).

(Bottom) Shades of gray lend to a nocturnal corner of the master bedroom. The painting (*Frayed Around The Edges*, 1975) is by Duggie Fields. The custom bed continues the indigo satin furniture story.

(Opposite) Inlay painted doors are echoed in authentic wood chair sides. The cabinet, built for the apartment, is made up of a series of cubes piled on top of each other. The Berber carpet was brought back from a trip to North Africa.

Freedom to feel unrestricted creatively is something I haven't had to fight for and that's a wonderful thing to be able to say. On this project, my client was particularly generous. She opened the door of the large white empty living room and said, "This is it. I'm confident you'll do something great." The offer was coming from someone who spent a good amount of time in museums, galleries, art institutions and at dance performances. Even her cat was named Merce, after the choreographer Merce Cunningham.

I looked around and, like always, went straight to the windows. There were beautiful old brownstones across the way. Immediately, I suggested bringing that architectural element into her room. Ironically, here we were in a glamorous apartment building and all I could think of were the funky old brownstones. She didn't even flinch.

Her aesthetic was based in simple, clean, classic-modern designs. She admired Mackintosh and Hoffman, and understood the importance of the Bauhaus and its influence. At the same time, she still hung on to a lot of possessions (that were in the rest of the apartment) that were family pieces, and the majority were heavy Victorian things.

A few days later, I presented her with the general concept and explained some of the references that would be incorporated. The fireplace, baseboards and some of the details in the room would be treated to look like the brownstones, which happened to be from the same Victorian Era

as some of her antiques. The corner support beams would have a sculptural quality informed by the work of Tony Smith. They would be done in black to give a strong upward thrust, but with a bit of veining to ease the severity.

The walls were made up of large flat panels surrounded by small moldings that would be perfect as "pre-fab" frames for pictures that could be done within them. A simple palette of muted tones, colors that we both really loved—grays, mauve, cream—would be used. Lissitzky and Moholy-Nagy paintings, photographs, and constructivist pieces would be reduced to simple shapes placed over each other creating subtle geometric silhouettes. Once painted, the details in the room would be similar to those in a Pompeian room, juxtaposed to the paintings within the flat panels.

I really only worked on the room a matter of days. Shortly after I finished, her contemporary Italian modern sofas arrived, and the Alvar Aalto table soon after. I was excited about them coming into the room. A few other pieces followed. Though stark, the room was complete and it had a nice balance between the popular minimalist industrial interior design movement at that time and the decorative approach that I was doing.

Our working relationship continued and I proceeded to help her in other areas of the apartment, although never with as much freedom as I was given in that main room. That had been such a special opportunity.

One result of having contacts in the fashion world was that my projects were always on a list of potential locations for photo shoots. There had already been a few sittings in this apartment and everything went without any trouble. During one particular session for *Vogue* magazine, the models, for some reason, were not wearing any clothing. It had something to do with a skin product campaign. To give a luminous, dewy quality, all of the girls were covered in a fine metallic powder. When the client got home she called me to say that on all of the black polished cotton sofas in the living room, there were imprints of the girls—like ghosts that had left their shadows everywhere. The magazine agreed to pay to have everything professionally cleaned, but we were always convinced that we could still see the impressions of the girls.

The owner and I have remained friends and I learned a valuable lesson in perseverance. After a financial loss, she went back to law school, joined a large, prestigious firm, and created a very different life for herself, always finding time to see the latest art exhibit or performance.

(Above) ART REFERENCE: *Free Ride*, Tony Smith (1962). The black steel of the Tony Smith sculpture informed the corner support pillars' vertical thrust and influenced the minimalist approach used in the living room-as-art-piece commission.

(Opposite) Photographer Deborah Turbeville took this photograph for *Vogue* magazine in 1979. The nude stands in repose against the painted brownstone-like mantel in this Upper West Side apartment. The female subjects are covered in metallic powdered makeup which left ghostly impressions on the black upholstered furniture.

(Above) Sparsely furnished, the living room's existing architectural details were individually picked out and embellished with painted techniques. Beyond the black polished cotton down-filled sofas, the brownstones that played a part in the inspiration for the interior loom across the way. Four Alvar Aalto tables are nested as one.

(Opposite Top) Narrow panels received fluted trompe l'oeil motifs. The plaster quarter-sphere lights, also treated to look like the brownstones, were incorporated. The existing wall moldings served as ready-made frames for mauve-and gray-colored flat planes to be painted within their boundaries.

(Opposite Bottom) ART REFERENCE: *House of Augustus, Room of the Masks, Rome* (200 A.D.). This reference photograph contributed to the decorative painting, particularly with its illusionistic architecture reduced to flat shapes and surfaces. The coloring and details are similar to the brownstones.

(This Page Top) Veining on the black support pillar eases the severity and brings it back to the Roman painting. The 1980s metal and lacquered wood Italian floor lamp blasts light when necessary.

(This Page Bottom) Rectangular panels serve as minimalist art. Upholstered furniture fits together or can be pulled apart like the shapes in the murals.

(Above) ART REFERENCE: *K VII*, Laszlo Moholy-Nagy (1922). This severely rectangular study served as a starting point for the panels within the room's moldings. Moholy-Nagy was one of a number of influential Bauhaus alumni, better known for his photographs.

(Opposite Top) The corner pillar appears to hold up the brownstone-painted support beams and crown moldings. Pairs of shapes play off each other in the flat panels. A sawhorse-style table base and modern version of a folding campaign chair with red lacquered metal frame add a touch of deep chroma color.

(Opposite Bottom) Mossy-gray cement-like paint ties together the baseboards, moldings, and flat areas of walls. The floors in deep walnut add a rich, traditional element to the room.

PRE-RAPHAELITE DECO
Upper East Side (Manhattan) · 1978

When asked how he became an art dealer, my next client answered, "it all started with the purchase of a Lalique vase, later traded for another more valuable object." Standing in this beautiful, old apartment, I realized how shrewd and clever he was. It was more like a warehouse repository in the beginning. I was commissioned to give a more suited background to the owner and his collection.

The rooms were more or less designated by the art and furniture that they contained. Few paintings were hung. Mostly they were stacked four- to- five deep on the floor along the walls. There were European paintings, particularly the Pre-Raphaelites and the Symbolists, next to paintings from the 1920s and 1930s. Museum-quality pieces of Art Nouveau furniture by Eugène Vallin and Charles Mackintosh sat next to an illuminated twentieth-century jukebox.

Categorizing everything was the first job, which wasn't that difficult except that the collector found the mix amusing. This was his home and he loved being surrounded by possessions that he considered to be his diverse friends. Without much convincing and for the sake of clarity for those coming to view the work, we did organize. This was done according to date and style. I called in a friend who was experienced with gallery installations to help with the hanging and placement of the art once the rooms had been decorated.

In most of the paintings there were dominant colors that were taken into account for use on the walls. My approach came more from the question, "What would Marcel Proust or Oscar Wilde have done?" Of course, the answer was lavender. This was the hue used for the entry hall and dining room gallery, as well as for the fabric of the window treatment. With hand-painted burnished gold crown moldings and the narrow fireplace mantel complete, we were now ready to arrange the furniture.

In the study, the work of English designer William Morris and his affection for natural motifs was the stylistic choice. Here, I was able to do some painting of my own. The wainscoting, doors, frames, and baseboards were done with glazes and layers of green woodgraining, giving substance without competing with the art and furnishings. Creamy silk-jersey fabric was stretched on wood doorframes and installed over the windows. The bottom section of fabric was gathered and the faux bois continued all around it. The walls were also in a light green (bordering on institutional) and did what that color always does—gave a fresh calming atmosphere to the room.

Calm was not my reaction when a delivery of wicker furniture, purchased at a flea market, arrived from France. Its woven material incorporated overscale arms in the shape of elephants, complete with wood tusks. The set was intended for the terrace but didn't fit. The owner decided it should stay in the study. While trying to keep a sense of humor (and the job), I had it painted in another shade of green, then gilded the tusks. Luckily my eye always went to the white Mackintosh chair and the amazing steel and glass ship's desk that conformed to the bay window.

Dusty rose (or deep flesh tone) went up on the bedroom walls. The former owner had a mirrored ceiling installed, which we considered removing until one of the spot bulbs from a torch lamp used while painting struck the mirror sending geometric patterns down over the room. The effect with the Cassandra posters and the French table seemed appropriate to the 1930s—as in a Marlene Dietrich movie. With the room complete and the arrival of a sensational Lempicka painting, we immediately hung the portrait of a woman in lace between two large mirrors.

Fortunately, photographs were taken of the apartment just after its completion, as the Tamara de Lempicka was sold shortly after it was put up. Although it was a private home, it was still that of a dealer who was in the business of buying and selling. Many years later I was at the Victoria and Albert Museum in London looking at the art of Edward Burne-Jones. I was amazed to think that I once had worked in such a close proximity that I could touch his painting—something I couldn't do in the museum.

(Above) ART REFERENCE: *Ophelia*, John Everett Millais (1851–52). *Ophelia* hearkens back to a time before the Age of Enlightenment, as with many of the works of art in the client's private collection.

(Opposite) Oscar Wilde's favorite lavender is used as a backdrop for the entrance and gallery artwork, including a poetic pastel by Rossetti, one of the Pre-Raphaelite Brotherhood. *Fantasie Egyptienne* by Charles Winter is framed within the arch. The room's height accommodates *St. Michael Slaying Satan* by Emile Fabry. A pair of Mackintosh chairs are used as extra seating in the dining room.

(Above) Formerly a repository, the dining room gallery appears to be a period piece after the renovation. The tables and chairs are by Eugène Vallin. The Burne-Jones paintings are stacked one on top of the other. Checkerboard wood floors are original to the old-world residence.

(Opposite Top) ART REFERENCE: *Portrait of the Duchess of Valmy*, Tamara de Lempicka (1924). The reference incorporates the curves of the earlier furniture as well as the art. Her skin tone was used as the wall color in the bedroom where a number of Lempicka paintings that the collector owned are hung.

(Opposite Middle) The French Art Nouveau cabinet by Hector Guimard hovers in the corner like a bat with widespread wings. On the cabinet is a precariously placed collection of art glass by Clément Massier.

(Opposite Bottom) A bronze and alabaster serpent floor lamp by Edgar Brandt rises above the room rimmed in precious objects.

(Pages 34–35) A Eugène Vallin table lamp imparts a glow in the evening. Four bent wood and leather chairs and the Art Deco carpet share their 1930s origins. The sunlight filters through silk jersey on custom wood doors. I was commissioned to paint the green wood graining covering the wainscoting, mantelpiece, and doors.

(Opposite Top) Art Nouveau candlesticks and ceramic sculpture rest on the mantel.

(Opposite Bottom) A Paris flea market wicker sofa lightens the seriousness of the subject matter in the paintings.

(Above) Charles Mackintosh designed this chair at the turn of the century. An American Arts & Crafts fire screen stands in front of one of the building's original wood and marble fireplaces.

(Opposite Top) Through the doorway of the bedroom stands the portrait of the young daughter of painter Tamara de Lempicka.

(Opposite Bottom) The numerous Cassandra posters above the American Art Deco limed oak table appear to be doubled in number by the mirror opposite. A Walter von Nessen chrome table lamp shares the tabletop with a Deco bronze streamline figure.

(Above) Chevron patterns are thrown from light reflecting off of the mirror. After an all too brief stay, the Lempicka was taken down and sold within days of the project's completion.

GRECO-ROMAN NEW YORK
Upper West Side (Manhattan) - 1979

The first time my friend Gaby brought me to meet her friend, a potential client, he was sitting at a table scattered with colorful Fiestaware plates and Clarice Cliff pottery. Whenever I visit a new place, my attention (no matter what is going on inside) always goes to the windows—partially to get a better sense of where I am, but also to check the light and to see the views if there are any. Next to the window there was a door. In front of the glass all I could see was foliage of various types. Walking out onto the large terrace, the whole of Central Park—its full expanse—was visible. My eye skimmed across the treetops, to the Metropolitan Museum, up to Harlem, and over to Central Park South. It occurred to me that this was the ultimate garden to have—plus you wouldn't need to tend it, as someone else would do it for you. Though the building was in disrepair and the apartment was a one bedroom and rather small, from this vantage point it all seemed very grand and very decadent. It was definitely New York, but felt more like being in ancient Rome or Athens during their heydays.

Back inside, the tea party was in full swing. There was conversation about mutual friends in London and New York, and who was doing what in fashion, advertising, hair and makeup. Throughout the chatter, film references kept coming up. At one point I heard the expression, "sword and sandal movie," and from then

on, I didn't hear much of anything else. This was the perfect place to create a hedonistic environment where pleasure would be the main thrust.

Rarely does this happen, but here I was pretty much given free rein as artist and designer. Once the design concept was made clear, we were full steam ahead. During this period, my interest in manipulating materials to look like something other than what they were was at its height. The first call to order was to paint the entire place in limestone colors that most think of as Classic—like the stones of the Parthenon, Concordia in Agrigento, Sicily, or older yet, the temples of Egypt. With the addition of sand to the paint and drawing fine lines to indicate seams, the walls and beams became large blocks of imaginary stone. With a wash of grime and painted green moss in the corners, the aging process was sped up.

There wasn't much furniture to worry about that the owner needed to keep, except a glass-topped American-Modern dining table which was placed on a raised platform and surrounded by custom-made banquettes constructed of wood done to perfection as huge chunks of granite. On top of linen cushions one could sit, sprawl out, or even lie down, while eating and drinking in sensuous epicurean abandon. And in fact, many nights were spent gathered around the table doing just that.

The bed was built in the same manner as the living room furniture with the same misunderstanding on the excellent carpenter's part (all of the pieces were delivered with clean, crisp edges that didn't add to the look of worn blocks as intended). So for days we cut, sanded, and generally abused them all before the granite finish was done. In addition to all of the theatricality, there was a practical side to this furniture. On each piece, invisible doors opened and enormous amounts of storage space was available. The floors throughout were sanded, then a translucent wash of color was pulled across the surface of the wood, again compelling the eye and the mind to question what material it truly was.

A conscious decision was made to keep the terrace floor clear and spacious. The high maintenance of the veranda in its former state was pared way down. The many bushes, trees, and planters overflowing with perennials were donated to the communal rooftop garden. Wooden dividing walls were erected at each end, serving as backdrops for the addition of a pair of Classical busts on cast cement columns. These pointed up the trees beyond. Now the park really was his private garden.

The working relationship crossed over, and the client became a friend. He was also instrumental in helping me to land other design projects, as well as ventures into commercial work (backdrops, sets, and showrooms for clothing designers). Many years later we worked together in this same location, creating a duplex after obtaining the apartment directly below his. The Fiestaware colors were put away for the Mediterranean banquets, but made a comeback in the new renovation.

(Above) ART REFERENCE: *Perspective View of the Sea Terrace*, Karl Friedrich Schinkel, Wilhelm Loeillot (1847). The caryatids in Schinkel's watercolor share a similar high vantage point to the Central Park West apartment. Greco-Roman art and architecture dominate the interior design.

(Opposite) The 1940s plaster frames are integrated into the surfaces of the walls. In this mélange of elements, the sconces incorporate silver leafing reflecting the installed lighting, and geometric hammered glass that diffuses the glare. Walls throughout are turned into large stone blocks with paint complete with faux moss.

(Opposite) Greco-Roman style dining and lounging takes place on the custom stone-like furniture surrounding a glass-topped American-Modern dining table. Doing as the Romans did, linen was chosen for the cushion coverings, hence the term "changing the linens." The real leopard-skin pillows were made from a vintage coat. The amphora is a twentieth-century Greek Revival piece on an onyx and bronze pillar. The nineteenth-century oil painting was based on a frieze from Herculaneum.

(Opposite Top) ART REFERENCE: *The Women of Amphissa*, Lawrence Alma-Tadema (1887). The painting served as the ultimate Olympian fantasy for the interior as well as the terrace. The subdued palette is in contrast to the brilliant colors in guests' wardrobes.

(Opposite Bottom) Stony shelving supported by cast columns in cement seems to transform collectibles into offerings to the gods. A photograph by Horst is next to a plaster cast of a figure in a draped toga.

(Above) The cantilevered shelf's edges were abused, then lovingly painted to evoke a well-worn slab of granite. Several 1920s campaign-style stools are scattered throughout. Dead space discovered behind the wall was used to create a niche with suspended glass shelves and storage for wine and spirits.

(Opposite) A sarcophagus-like bed faces the morning sun and views of the museum across the park. An impeccably well-done bronze and marble tripod from the nineteenth century serves as a night table.

(Top) The flat areas of the ceiling, in silver leaf, were allowed to tarnish. The crossbeams take on extra weight visually with their stone technique.

(Middle) Numerous potted plants were eliminated to point up Central Park as the client's personal garden. The stone muse keeps a fixed gaze toward Central Park South. Her mate faces north. Custom wood walls were created to divide the long terrace. The reservoir in the background glistens on sunny mornings.

(Bottom) One of the client's prized possessions is this bronze male sculpture from the Victorian era on soft pink marble. A second wall sconce (one of three) adorns and illuminates the textured wall.

The desired result with this interior was to turn the key and allow feelings to move where the characters in Watteau's paintings reside. The small but well-proportioned apartment was located on what was becoming a very familiar stretch of Central Park West (I had already completed three projects there previously).

Themes and historical references seemed to dominate my early work. A large part of my choices also stemmed from the owners. This client had a wonderful, playful, opulent side to his personality, complete with dousing himself in much fragrance. This was someone who would be open to the curves and tendrils of the Baroque and Rococo periods, providing it was done with a contemporary eye.

The windows looking out over the park were positioned at roughly eye level. This allowed an immediate viewing of the profusion of flowering trees in the spring. Central Park is similar in design to the gardens surrounding the Petit Trianon, with their new change toward an English style of landscaping (lakes, rocks, irregular curves, temples, and statues). Thinking in these terms would enhance the interiors, adding the extra dimension of the park as a garden.

In Paris, it isn't unusual to see beautiful detailing even in a modest abode. Tall glass French doors as windows, antique mantels for the fireplace, and wood paneling in lieu of plain plaster walls are often part of domestic Parisian life. In America, we don't necessarily have these luxuries built in. So, when discovering a pair of spectacular, eighteen-foot-tall, French château doors, the client and I were determined to have them as part of his place. The rest of the elements would have to be included in the furnishings and suggested in the treatment of the surfaces. The small, average interior doors were removed and the walls closed up. A floor-to-ceiling portal was created and the Rococo doors installed. These were inset with mirrors on one side and the panels were edged with leaves on the other—all in remarkable condition given

their considerable age. A trip to theMetropolitan Museum of Art to look at the European period rooms, and thinking about how we could adapt some of what we were swooning over, helped the process. From then on, there was no trepidation about the direction we were heading.

What I enjoy the most is testing new decorative painting techniques and putting my personal stamp on interior design projects. The floors were sanded, bleached, and stained light blonde. Together with my painting protégé, Erik Filban, we traced and painted a round medallion in a Boucher blueish-green in the center of the main room. Clear varnish protected the floors and the motif giving a satin sheen throughout. The walls were painted an ivory; they then received a pale striped striation in a deeper shade. Tone-on-tone coloring was everywhere—walls, furniture, banquette cushions, chair seats, and ceilings. As a departure, in the bathroom glass sections were measured for the top half of the walls, then painted in a reverse-glass technique depicting underwater scenes. Silver leaf was applied and the glass installed. The end result was like being submerged in Neptune's world of coral, plants, mermaids and exotic fish. Villa Trianon and Elsie de Wolfe stylistically guided the way. The scale was small, but the impact was great, calming, and luxurious.

Metallic gold gleamed away on the round tea table base in the living room. Gilded bronze candelabrum lamps were the main source of light, accentuating the leafed details on the eighteenth-century wood-and-gesso mirror frame. The fancy and the fanciful were eased a bit with a distressed paint-flaking table placed under the large mirror. A well-worn marble exterior bench served as a coffee table in front of the low seating that extended the width of the room.

Before closets, there were armoires. Thank the decorating gods for these. The apartment's lack of closets was easily dealt with. Shops with large, beautiful cabinets, dressers, night tables, and the like were not difficult to come by in 1980s Manhattan. The piece we chose had a very architectural quality, similar to a model of a Beaux Arts building. It housed bed linens, towels, napkins and tablecloths, many personal items and, back to modern reality, the media equipment.

The owner also discovered fantastic items and always included me before making a final decision, which is something most designers really appreciate. Some of his finds included a very large carved head of the Chinese goddess Guan Yin, and a pair of nine-foot-tall light-wood fluted columns with attached urn at the top from the 1930s.

Though shocking to our color palette, a vintage magenta silk curtain for the bedroom was picked up at a flea market. I trust Lady Mendl (or Ms. de Wolfe) would have approved. Sheer linen gauze hung on a single, pale-wood pole. This afforded some sense of privacy. In the bedroom, the thick-lined curtain could be pulled across to block the light, readying the room for sleeping in, or a dangerous liaison.

Shortly after we finished, the client went on to a very demanding career that required being on location in various parts of the world for long periods of time. With the purchase of a house in England, this New York set of rooms became his pied-à-terre.

(Above) ART REFERENCE: A Meeting in a Park, Jean Antoine Watteau (1712–1713). The pursuits in the aptly titled Rococo painting parallel what still occurs beyond the windows of the Central Park West apartment. These are the characters that were imagined as the apartment's occupants.

(Opposite) The gilded bronze lighting is bounced back by the gold leaf of the mirror and metallic printed fabric on the Louis XVI armchair. A large botanical medallion was hand-painted on the center of the living room floor.

(Page 50 Top Left) A Rococo-style chandelier is reflected in the distressed mirror panels on the door of the bedroom armoire.

(Page 50 Top Right) The elaborate cast-bronze candelabrum (one of a pair) was updated with electrical wiring.

(Page 50 Bottom Left) A Victorian version of a Rococo table base was capped with round leafed-wood. An anonymous woman gazes out from an eighteenth-century portrait in a gilded frame, hanging on the hand-painted, striated walls.

(Page 50 Bottom Right) A Beaux Arts armoire brings together bold, diverse elements in one extremely practical piece for the bedroom. In the foreground, the original hardware of the doors is visible.

(Page 51) In an attempt to replicate a French interior, a pair of doors from a French château were incorporated running from floor to ceiling, changing the apartment radically.

(Opposite Top) It is just a few short steps from the apartment to the wonders of Central Park where oaks appear to be enormous candelabra.

(Opposite Bottom) The interior seems more spacious seen through mirror images. The 1930s light wood fluted column and urn are illuminated from within.

(Above) A custom low banquette runs from one end to the other, making the turn to touch the door. An antique marble garden bench provides a surface while lounging. Soft metallic leaves are printed on the cushion fabric and are similar in appearance to the foliage outside through the linen gauze curtains.

(Opposite Top) Ever-changing tablescapes with romantic references are subjects for paintings themselves.

(Opposite Middle) In the master bath, period sconces sit over the verre églomisé (reverse painted glass) underwater motifs created for the walls.

(Opposite Bottom) Distressed flaking paint on the table and mirror lends a sense of passing time and history.

(Above) The Chinese head of the Goddess of Mercy, Guan Yin, vies for attention with the Bacchus divinely decadent French bronze lamp. The armoire holds a multitude of linens as well as modern necessities.

VENETIAN ARCHES
Upper West Side (Manhattan) - 1981

Everything was too familiar in the prewar "Old New York style" apartment. Although we had seen it through a number of decorating schemes, always featuring creativity and innovation like its occupant, change was imminent. Upon hearing that a remarkable apartment was becoming available a few flights above, the client jumped at the opportunity to see it. And it was remarkable. The place had been used as a dance studio. Critical walls had been removed. The kitchen and bathroom were neglected and there were damaged surfaces everywhere. Focusing on the potential and not the enormous task ahead, we committed to the renovation then and there.

The former apartment had no light or views, but this set of rooms was flooded with morning sun and faced one of the most breathtakingly detailed façades in New York City. From this vantage point, a mix of sixteenth-century French Renaissance, Gothic forms, and Italian Renaissance ornament all added up to something quite Venetian in appearance. There were enough components in the new apartment that shared this extravagant mix. As a result, we knew which direction to take the interior design.

Having recently completed a project with designer Stephen Shadley, this was another opportunity for us to continue our working relationship. We teamed up to bring the apartment back to its former glory. With a fastidious contractor the work began.

The owner of Second Hand Rose, the legendary designer resource, had spared from the Dumpster a number of architectural items removed before the demolition of a 1920s Brooklyn movie palace. With their fragile beauty, three gilded wood-and-gesso pointed arches that had once framed the doorways in the theater were the perfect way to embellish the openings to the living room and dining room in the

apartment. In lieu of the fourth arch, the entrance to the bedroom hallway was created in plaster to repeat the same silhouette.

We attempted to stay true to the authenticity of the building and the spirit of a palazzo throughout the seven rooms. Even a new kitchen incorporating original wood and glass cabinets along with modern appliances still looked like it belonged. The master bath retained its massive undulating tub and sink. Black-and-white checkerboard mosaic tile ran through on the floor of the service entrance and kitchen. The window treatment started out with simple translucent soft Roman shades, but ultimately upholstered pelmets and hotel-like drapery in vivid red and raw sienna cotton velvet were added increasing the luxurious, old world ambience.

Above the wainscoting in the two main rooms, we had the paper hanger dress up the walls with individual alternating squares of neutral-toned grass cloth, producing a subtle checkerboard pattern. As if stepping out of a time machine into the 1930s, the rooms suddenly had a touch of the modernism of designer Jean-Michel Frank. Although generally associated with the 1960s, long shaggy carpeting had been used in a number of rooms by another decorating mentor, Syrie Maugham, much earlier in the 1920s. We used it in the center of the living room floor rimmed with a flat velvet carpet as a play on textures. Continuing along these lines, plush moss fringe bordered out all of the cushions on the flat linen slipcovered sofas. One more addition to the era was added when the client returned from a trip to Paris with a three-tiered alabaster hanging light fixture that was featured in the center of the room.

I stopped in my tracks upon spotting a metal light fixture in a shop on Elizabeth Street. Like overscaled jewelry, I thought that the sculptural series of metal ribs would be the perfect focal point for the dining room. Happily the client thought so too. The jewelry theme was continued with two custom steel and granite square tables. Their stone tops were held up and supported by strategic vertical points on the base, as in a ring with a prong setting. Somewhere between yellow and green, chartreuse velvet covered the chairs from a local thrift shop, which were originally made in the 1960s, but appeared to be earlier in style. The chairs were placed on three sides of the table, while a long upholstered banquette served the fourth side. For dinner parties, guests graciously allowed each other to scoot in and out. This setup made the room far more intimate and interesting than strictly using chairs.

The owner's parents were avid auction-house hunters. As a result we had access to fabulous antiques and paintings that could have come straight out of a Venetian villa. These included a carved blackamoor holding up a swagged, draped console and Dutch portraits in ebonized frames. There was even a large, beautifully painted copy of a Rubens that featured Venus being offered a misshapen Baroque pearl. All these and more found a spot somewhere in the interior.

I've often heard people lament when seeing the extraordinary, "that could never be done these days." Here, the combination of ideas and fine craftsmanship was on par with the excellence of another era. The final outcome was that everything new was old again.

(Above) ART REFERENCE: *The Libreria*, John Singer Sargent (1904). The study by John Singer Sargent painted during a trip to Venice parallels the interior design and original detailing both inside and outside of the prewar apartment.

(Opposite) In the foreground of the bedroom hallway hangs a large nineteenth-century reproduction of a Rubens acquired at an auction in the 1950s. The pointed arch was made with plaster, repeating the shape of the arches salvaged from a Brooklyn movie palace. The highly reflective, ebonized floors throughout bounce the light. One of six dining chairs purchased at a thrift store belies its age.

(Opposite) A play in textures, long threaded wool carpet and the bushy moss fringe on the cushions are balanced by flat grass cloth wall coverings hung in alternating directions. The alabaster tiered light fixture was hand-carried onto a plane from Paris.

(Top) Out the window is one of New York's most arresting façades. Impossible to compete with, we played along with its extravagance in the apartment's interior.

(Bottom) The wood-and-gesso pointed arches that came from an elaborate movie theater received a new life framing the openings in the renovated prewar home. The return edges were hand-gilded with sheets of gold leaf adding more substance.

59

(Top) A relief from the weighty overscaled appointments, delicate glass vessels dance across the table.

(Bottom) A number of framed caricatures appear thrown across the vintage grass cloth wall covering illuminated by a vintage Venetian glass lamp. A table and curvy chairs provide a spot off of the kitchen to review recipes and have a coffee.

(Opposite) Impossible to manage one enormous sheet of granite, a pair of tables was fabricated to resemble a ring's prong setting. The metal ceiling light fixture is French and reminiscent of a Louise Bourgeois spider sculpture, or the ribs of a Tyrannosaurus rex.

(Above) The bed is Venetian, painted wood with grotesques and putti. The ethereal window curtains were hand-painted, marbleized silk.

(Opposite Top) ART REFERENCE: *Universal Harmony*, Paolo Veronese (1561). The Veronese detail encapsulates the opulence and sophistication of a Venetian palazzo we were striving for in the apartment.

(Opposite Bottom) Purchased at an auction in the 1950s, this ebony figure holding a silver platter is in keeping with our inspirational mentor, Syrie Mougham, and her use of blackamoors.

ORIENTALIST SANCTUARY
Gramercy (Manhattan) -1982

Calling from his new apartment, a friend from Great Britain commented, "I don't have many possessions since moving to New York except an Orientalist watercolor that has little to do with my new place, but you will see."

When we entered the converted church rectory hall, my work partner at the time, Stephen Shadley, and I were struck at the sight of a huge stained glass window—this was only the top half. The floor severed it in the middle; the bottom was the downstairs neighbor's.

The three of us discussed the scope of the work and somehow the conversation shifted to Seville, Spain, and Istanbul, Turkey, and to churches converted into mosques, the most famous being the Hagia Sophia. I tried to put into words how phenomenal it was that each transition allowed the last

to still exist. We took a risk and decided this was the route to take for the interior. Later, taking time from his demanding career, he approved the direction we were heading and gave us his blessings to move forward.

Standing on top of a high ladder, I applied cement-like paint covering the areas between the leaded glass windows. The arch shape was accentuated with two-tone striped blocks, appearing Romanesque or North African. The remarkable finished effect was as though we were looking at the exterior of a building. From that point the room felt like a large terrace. To emphasize this, we continued by installing a huge figurative bas-relief that might have been part of an early church facade.

Privacy was achieved in the sleeping quarters above the bath and kitchen with a custom-designed movable window. This was the opposite of the main window but we selected similar materials and some of the same colored glass. It was sort of Mondrian meets Notre Dame Cathedral.

We avoided the use of jewel colors generally associated with what we Westerners think of as "Oriental." All of the furniture in the main room was upholstered in Belgian linen with a few exceptions. For fun, a pair of stools and a Mies van der Rohe Barcelona chair were done in a sumptuous leopard velvet fabric (a textile that would make its way into many of my interiors).

Everybody laughed when I said, "we simply must have some damask!" An extremely tall folding screen was made to include this crucial element, typical of Spain and Turkey. It held its own standing next to the large window. On guard around the room, beautifully crafted Italian floor lamps stood on the gleaming ebonized wood floor—not only for illumination, but also to pick up the leaded patterns appearing in the windows. We were encouraged to continue with additional custom designs, and continue we did.

Bringing together this theatrical environment would have intimidated some, but that was not the case here. The occupant of this apartment, like the Orientalist watercolor, made perfect sense in this space after all. The painting now belongs to another friend and client. Its magic is still working.

(Above) ART REFERENCE: *A Memlook Bey, Egypt*, John Frederick Lewis (1868). The self-portrait of the nineteenth-century English artist known for his Orientalist paintings was much appreciated by the British client. His works formed the basis of the design.

(Opposite) The Celtic pattern in the floor lamps also appears in the leaded glass window. A set of Spanish chairs upholstered in artist's canvas adds character but remain neutral. An antique bejeweled saber is positioned over a chest from Spain. The palm fronds in the Victorian glass vessel add an exotic touch.

(Above) The room's centerpiece stained glass window as seen from the exterior.

(Below) ART REFERENCE: A *Trade on the Beach*, Frank Brangwyn (1892). While working on the studio we identified with the Belgian-born artist, Brangwyn, looking for inspiration in North Africa and the East.

(Opposite) A soaring room resulted from the conversion of the nineteenth-century parish hall. It serves as a living room, dining room, and an open guest room. All of the furnishings are united by an ebony stained floor which severs the enormous window in half. Holding its own while contributing a sense of mystery and the imperative Venetian damask fabric, the folding screen can be pulled across to control the natural light. The use of plush leopard velvet gives the Barcelona chair a different connotation.

(Opposite) A custom asymmetrically patterned glass door provides privacy. It pivots out into the main room from the sleeping loft. When hosting guests, the overscaled daybed provides a luxurious place to sleep. The cast of a panel from Luca della Robbia's bas-relief, Cantoria, is placed on the outside of the ochre-colored kitchen wall. The shield and swords are eighteenth-century Persian. A pair of stools found in a consignment shop were reupholstered to look like cats.

(Above) The sunken foyer is used as a small library. The room is kept purposely dark, illuminated by a sole filigree fixture heightening the experience when stepping up into the main room. The client's nineteenth-century painting attributed to John Frederick Lewis took temporary residence here.

(Below) ART REFERENCE: Whirling Dervishes, Jean-Léon Gérôme (1899). The motivation to include Persian swords came directly from the collection in the Gérôme painting. The dervish's tennure, or dress, in solid white is represented by the white canvas of the furnishings.

Middleton Gardens and Drayton Hall, once plantations, formed my impressions of Charleston, South Carolina, during my first visit in the early 1980s. This Southern city is layered in history. In my imagination, its columned buildings, sphagnum moss-hung live oak trees, and Civil War ruins evoke architect Piranesi's idealized drawings of ancient Rome.

On that trip, during an outdoor concert I was offered a slice of cake by a charismatic woman who had seen some of my work and intended to contact me to help update her family home. Back in New York, I did get the phone call as promised. It was a simple starting point for a long-standing multifaceted relationship.

Facing the Battery, the house was by Charleston standards a more recent one from 1918—even oddly referred to as "new." In collaboration with fellow artist/designer Stephen Shadley and painter Erik Filban, we came up with a renovation and decoration plan that was accepted with only minor changes.

We entered the city ready to attack with paintbrushes and concept boards in hand. Met by enthusiastic clients and masters of hospitality, we began to work and enjoy being in this special part of America. Within days we assembled a local team including a contractor, paper hangers, upholsterers and metalworkers who were happy to be working for the designers from "Off," as we were referred to (because we were not locals). This proved to be an asset as they were more than aiming to please.

The work was temporarily interrupted as we were summoned to take part in the yearly festival of the arts. Concerts, exhibits, operas, dance performances, and parties stimulated us as our host, a Spoleto board member, led the way.

In the houses that were considerably older and particularly noteworthy architecturally, a way of decorating and furnishing had been established and remained prevalent. Although we appreciated this traditional style, our clients and their house would allow for something much more dramatic that would set it apart from the rest. A theatrical approach was certainly atypical for Charleston residences. No Waterford chandelier here. An alabaster and bronze Greco-Roman light fixture would dominate the entrance seating area. Above the original mantel with its carved procession of draped figures, another diaphanously clothed female symbol of music—an architectural detail spared from a demolished theater—served as a focal point. The entire room was reflected in a Federal convex mirror that acted like a surveillance eye. An eclectic mix of period styles made up the furnishings—some heirlooms, others bought locally, and the more attention-grabbing pieces shipped from New York.

The classical motifs continued throughout, including the adjacent library and in the dining room with its painted murals. Switching from designers to painters we treated the room to look like eighteenth-century wallpaper, and again Piranesi's influence cannot be mistaken. A mixture of Roman themes and imagined scenes from local landscapes paralleled each other, complete with architectural ruins, waterways, and swamplands. Delighted with the hands-on approach, we were encouraged by the owners to continue with additional decorative painting. A sponge technique was used on the walls of the library giving the look of the inner pages of an old leather-bound book.

As the floors were being sanded, a series of medallions based on Robert Adam designs were drawn up, then transferred to the raw wood. Carefully brushed layers of varnish within the circular and octagonal motifs preserved the wood's lightest shade. Then, the floor refinishers applied their ebony stain and the patterns remained in sharp contrast to the rest of the floors. Once the final finish was done they appeared to be inlay of various types of wood.

As part of jazzing up the library, a spiral columned printed fabric was used on the sofa, the room's details were accentuated in glossy white paint, and the bookcase wall was embellished with pilasters, capitals, and architectural fragments also in white. These are all the elements that may be found in a Louise Nevelson sculpture. A custom art piece by Cletus Johnson (a box containing similar miniature building elements to ours) was hung dead center among the books, while a second piece with classical motifs was placed over the mantel. Coincidentally, we were then informed that the artist had actually worked intimately with the great Nevelson on her later pieces.

The warmth and humor of our patrons carried through the process making the time pass swiftly. After the first phase of the work was complete, we celebrated back at Middleton Gardens where we attended the closing ceremony for the Spoleto Festival. This was not the end. Work has continued over the years including bedroom renovations, a custom kitchen and an onyx-sheathed bathroom.

The classical references that were used here, like the friendships that were formed from that encounter, are what I still hold most dear.

(Above) ART REFERENCE: *Prima Parte: Title Page – State*, Giovanni Piranesi (1743). Piranesi's masterful skill at engraving architecture also introduced groups of vases, altars, and tombs that were often absent in reality. This was the artistic license we used for the rooms of this house in the Deep South.

(Opposite) The drawing room and main entrance are joined as one room. The furnishings combine Empire chairs, a Sheraton sofa, and a 1930s iron and slate table—all on a dark mahogany stained floor. The custom wood window cornices are embellished with a series of classical motifs taken from Pompeian wall paintings. A former bank light fixture in bronze and alabaster dominates. The frame of the Federal convex mirror includes candlesticks and a carved fawn reclining under a palm tree.

(Top Left) A live oak tree and Camellia bushes filter the sunlight outside of the library window.

(Top Right) In the vestibule the reflection of a pair of gesso-and-wood Italian Rococo consoles and mirrors creates a view of infinity. The walls are painted in artificial stone blocks with creeping fig growing from the illusionistic mortar.

(Bottom) A circle of dancing putti in Italian oil painting is hung over an illuminated nineteenth-century satyr and cherub bronze sculpture. Diverse furnishings include a folding American card table, a pair of Spanish hall chairs, and looming in the background a terra-cotta urn sitting on a corbel.

(Opposite) In the second-floor hallway, filtered light from the floor-to-ceiling window falls on Audubon's 1827 *American Crow* and a Carolina Low-Country chest of drawers originally from Hampton Plantation, the estate of poet laureate Archibald Rutledge.

(Above) The French 1930s crystal sailing vessel later replaced the silver Federal-style chandelier (see opposite page) for extra drama.

(Below) The English sideboard and tea set and Colonial candlesticks are a sampling of the house's extensive collection. The Roman goddess in the wall painting is entangled in creeping fig vine (a local invasive plant).

(Opposite) Roman themes with imagined scenes from local landscapes were painted above the tall wainscoting in the dining room by the designers. An English dining table placed diagonally allows for groups of eight or more.

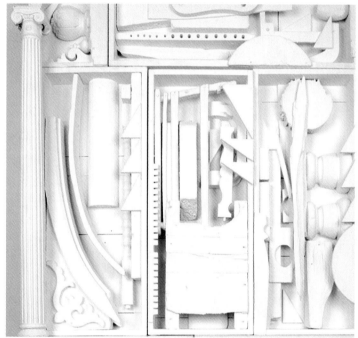

(Top) A cabinetmaker added architectural details to the bookcases. *Judy's Theatre* by Cletus Johnson incorporates miniature building materials into a custom shadow box.

(Middle) ART REFERENCE: *Dawns Wedding Chapel I*, Louise Nevelson (1959). In the Nevelson sculpture, found objects coexist to create a unified whole. In the library, intentionally placed pilasters, capitals, over-door fragments, accentuated dental moldings, a wood mantelpiece, and the column-printed fabric all mimic Nevelson's piece.

(Bottom) Bold patterns enliven the library. An Italian marble table rests on the 1930s floral-bordered American carpet. A pair of vintage leather and paisley chairs accompany a set of wood painted dummy boards (women's home companions) flanking the fireplace.

(Opposite) The circular floor medallion is based on a design by Robert Adam. A second Cletus Johnson construction, *Minerva*, is hung above the mantel. Graphic design sofa fabric appears to be a balustrade from behind.

(Above) An alabaster Swedish light fixture hangs in the theatrical bedroom hideaway. Another old Audubon print, this time of parrots, is placed smack-dab over floral textile. The 1940s Hollywood glamour Greek key motif mirror dominates and keeps the Classical theme going.

(Below) Custom black granite and ebonized cabinets fill the kitchen and breakfast room. The top reflects American silver and beyond it the lush gardens.

(Opposite) An ebonized Empire sleigh bed, bronze urn-shaped lamps and a pair of Swedish Beidermeier night tables are symmetrically placed in front of a pair of plantation shutters. A George Catlin print floats above the bed. Latin script appears to be written in stone on the European squares. A nineteenth-century painting of a young woman in fancy dress was purchased in Charleston.

WEST SIDE DISTRESS
TriBeCa (Manhattan) - 1984

For a number of years while my brother and I lived on Park Avenue, I would commute to a studio in TriBeCa, going from the sublime to the ridiculous, never quite sure which was which. When I first looked for a studio to work in, somewhere light, quiet, spacious, and affordable was the dream. An old brick turn-of-the-century building located on Greenwich Street below Canal, facing the Hudson River, appealed to me. Approaching the eccentric owner of what was formerly a storehouse for tins of Danish sugar cookies, I was told that indeed I could have a space in the building. He was even willing to install a bathroom and kitchen. Within months I was in what was to become known as "artists' housing."

Initially, the big single room was void of furniture. It was there that large canvases were stretched and personal artwork, photographer's backdrops, props, and decorative murals were done. It also served as a location for photo shoots.

The downtown west side, shortly after the completion of the Twin Towers, was in decline and decay. The city's progress, as well as its downturn, was visible from the windows of my studio. When a warehouse was demolished, excavators unearthed the remains of an eighteenth-century iron foundry. Close by, a slave burial site was discovered. Primarily the discovery and excavation are what sparked my imagination. This was happening at the same time I was learning more about the eighteenth-century excavators of Pompeii and Herculaneum. It was then that a wide range of historical references started to work their way into the interior space.

Making the parallel between Pompeii and New York as capitals of pleasure and sophistication, I began to concentrate on the motifs that would dominate the ceilings, floors, and a series of bricked-up arches that interrupted the walls. The first literal interpretation was a dark, nocturnal fresco painted within one of the arches. This seemed to visually break through the added brick and provided for my version of the ghostly deteriorating piers outside. On the opposite side of the room, another bricked-up arch suggested dawn, also freely adapted from Mediterranean wall paintings. The remaining areas within the arches were done extremely theatrically, using details from Federico Fellini's acclaimed film, *Satyricon*, as a starting point.

Once, fifty large wooden beams ran across the ceiling holding up the floor above. Much attention and care was given to the wood surface but regrettably soundproofing and a ceiling had to be installed. Although the otherworldly environment that was created cast a spell, the distractions of the neighbors ultimately became intolerable. Many layers of stucco-like paint were applied to the ceiling and ran down over the brick walls adding to an overall grotto effect. The writer Herbert Muschamp pointed out, "that while other loft dwellers were removing paint and plaster to expose brick, I was exposing my imagination on all the surfaces of the loft."

Layers of commercial grade plywood made up the floor— yet another opportunity to transform one material into another. Here, various techniques were utilized to give the appearance of terrazzo with marble chips, encased in cement and polished. The center of the floor included a painted rendition of an impluvium (a small pool where rainwater collected through the roof opening in the courtyard of a Roman villa). This proved to be all too realistic. Over the years, whenever the forecast was for severe showers, nerves would fray. The entire building leaked like a sieve.

As part of the conversion from studio to loft, a crew attached white porcelain tiles to make up the back wall of the open kitchen. My friend and painting colleague, Erik Filban and I took a hammer to the top rows of tile before marbleizing them in the most literally painted area of the place. We then added a frieze, more painted illusionary architecture, and a wooden shelf running from end to end. The area mimicked an ancient bakery. None of the painting was intended to represent the original pristine versions, but the petrified ones surviving the devastation in those doomed cities along the Mediterranean.

Although somewhat delusional, I pictured myself as dispossessed nobility reduced to residing in ruins over centuries. It was for the bed that this opera-like scenario's big aria was played

(Above) ART REFERENCE: *Frescoed Wall of the Triclinium 'C,'* from Villa Farnesina (19 B.C.). The mysterious, predominantly black detail painted in the Third style was a continuous source of inspiration for the loft.

(Opposite) Metal shutters on the exterior, as well as the interior, when shut protect from the elements in the former warehouse. In the foreground, the cast cement 1920s figure of Leda and the Swan is, although nude, slightly Archaic in detailing. Stacks of commissioned decorative panels from photo shoots for clients such as Bergdorf Goodman, CBS Records, and La Prairie form a backdrop.

out. Sections of a paneled room from Brittany—openings for cupboard beds that required climbing up into—were assembled. The pieces were attached to a raised platform, now a room within a room. Once up on the mattress, the view of the river was framed through the low carved headboards. The end result was something similar to a bed that may have been part of a set for a Puccini opera.

Fewer canvases were being painted in the loft. The majority of the work was now happening as commissions in patrons' homes. Furniture, practical and impractical, made its way in. Steering away from the obvious Empire Campaign furniture, chaise longue, and all the beautiful pieces that were being used in the revival of Neoclassicism, I selected items from other historical periods (Medieval French, Renaissance Italian, all the way to Art Deco New York). This helped to make a visual connection across time and place. These diverse layers referred not only to a series of changes in the decorative arts, but to my enthusiasm to extract something from every period, celebrating civilizations and their achievements. I was hard-pressed to find the same excitement in the progress that followed in lower Manhattan.

The changes were drastic and swift. Two large office towers went up in the lot in front of the building. Rents quadrupled and eviction notices on neighbors' doors were a common sight. What had been neglected was now prized. Developers moved in and artists were replaced by young, upwardly mobile professionals.

The kiss of death in my eyes was when the cobblestone streets were blacktopped over and the large curved steel Richard Serra sculpture was removed from the Holland Tunnel roundabout. Although minor details, these were symbolic of the passing of an era. Gratefully, the list of requirements that I had going into finding my ideal artist's studio on many levels were met. I did enjoy the sunsets, the river views, the relative quiet, and the ridiculously low rent for almost three decades, but I knew that like those living in the shadow of Vesuvius, I was on borrowed time.

(Pages 82–83) During the last days of TriBeCa as artists' housing, the former painting studio's motifs moved through a succession of periods from ancient Rome (walls) through Medieval France (stone table), Renaissance Italy (chair), up to Art Deco New York (hanging light fixture) and beyond.

(Opposite) Within the bricked-up arch, a painting based on the Third style of Roman wall frescoes is a ghostly rendition of the deteriorating pier in the Hudson. Three-hundred-year-old wood wall panels from Brittany were reconfigured as headboards for the raised steps allowing a view of evening sunsets. A Corinthian capital is used as a keystone.

(*Opposite*) In lieu of a volcanic eruption, the porcelain tile was thoughtfully broken, while large cracks and missing sections of the kitchen wall mural suggest the devastation. Art Deco hanging light fixtures formerly illuminated the ground floor of Macy's department store.

(*Above*) As in ancient times, the actual Bosc pears, real alabaster bowl, and marble tabletop are fitting subject matter for a still life.

(Opposite Top Left) ART REFERENCE: *Basket of Fruit*, Caravaggio (1600–1601). To my eye, the basket of fruit in the painting by Caravaggio could have been a detail in a Roman wall painting, 1500 years earlier.

(Opposite Top Right) A black1960s gold-veined marble boomerang serves as a counter. The tablescape consists of an amphora found beneath the sea off of Corsica, lemons arranged in an antique marble mortar from France, and a vintage photograph of a Diaghilev dancer from the 1920s.

(Opposite Bottom) Incorporating Caravaggio's use of chiaroscuro lighting, the detail from one of my figurative paintings echoes the shadows on the limbs and feet of the cast stone statue.

(Above) Layers of paint give a stucco texture to the brick walls. A collection of 1960s ceramic lamp bases are lined up as in a Giorgio Morandi study. The antlers are from Sri Lanka.

(Right) Beneath the iron table is my painted interpretation of an impluvium (a shallow pool in a Roman villa where rainwater was allowed to fall through and collect). Nineteenth-century objects appear suspended on the table's glass surface. An ancient small Roman bronze figure gestures as in a later dance by Isadora Duncan.

There was a very real connection from the start with this client. My working partner at the time, Stephen Shadley, and I were recommended by notable writer and journalist Patricia Warner. It didn't take too long to discover a shared passion for artifacts of all types, based in many cultures. The more that we learned about her multicultural background, the more it made sense.

We met at the newly acquired apartment and before discussing much of anything about the renovation, the owner insisted that we light incense, clap our hands, and pop Chinese firecrackers to frighten bad omens out of the windows. Rather than being put off by this, it contributed to my desire to work with her and gratefully, we did.

The building was from the late 1920s, close to Central Park but with no views of it or much of anything else. Two redeeming qualities of the apartment were a good amount of space and ample natural light. These could be further enhanced with the removal of some of the walls and by expanding the openings to the major rooms, which is what was done. Private suites were formed for the lady and young man of the house. When the client expressed her dislike for Sheetrock, real plaster walls would

be the only practical alternative. This is when visions of the Rothko Room at the Tate Modern, with its series of atmospheric paintings, and being surrounded by colored, modeled walls sprang to mind. We would keep the focus inward and create a sanctuary, in design and ambience.

The demolition was extensive and all of the walls were stripped down to the base layer. Even the fireplace mantel and everything from the original kitchen were pulled out. Throughout the process amongst the dust and debris, quartz crystals and bits of amethyst appeared on window ledges placed by the owner and her nine-year-old son. This was to ensure that positive energy was allowed to flow.

Many of the initial ideas came from a book with photographs that we were enamored with on the seventeenth-century Katsura Villa in Japan. In keeping with this, and to give intimacy to the foyer and dining room, shoji-type sliding screens were installed, replacing the former walls. The windows also received large panels, this time doors that swung open. Textured Plexiglas was used in place of the traditional rice paper in large sections. Instead of a customary mantel, three thick pieces of American bluestone (or slate) were assembled, two sides and a top, appearing more like an altar table. This was attached to the wall in front of the fireplace opening. The fire happened within this table and the warmth of one of many beautiful old figures of the Buddha radiated on top.

The kitchen incorporated a long, low wall made entirely of cement. It encased the stove and oven and hid other appliances from view. The floors were also done in concrete. Both were rubbed with a pale moss green pigment and then sealed. There were cabinets with mostly open shelving with one in particular that ran around the top of the entire room where functional and precious objects were on view. A long wood table and bench gave the feeling of being in a monastery where food was prepared.

Two enthusiastic artisans were brought in even as construction continued. They would be doing the fresco finish in the foyer, living room, and a few choice areas throughout. Rather than plaster and paint, these walls were treated with layers of fresh plaster with various colors in it to give a mesa quality. In addition to verbal instructions, photographic reproductions of Mark Rothko paintings and images of the striation in the Grand Canyon walls were followed as guides. Using shades of yellow ochre, raw sienna, and unbleached titanium all in a horizontal direction gave the desired effect. Glancing down, I noticed the reference pictures were also covered in a layer of plaster. As they were quick studies, the artisans no longer needed them.

Although the walls almost glowed from within and a final waxing bounced light, more luminosity and embellishment were desired. I proposed covering the flat panels in the ceiling of the living room in sheets of silver leaf. The client gave the go-ahead and I had a chance to engage in the hands-on approach that was prevalent in every project. With my painter friend, Erik Filban, we snapped gridlines and then bent over backward applying 2,500 sheets of four-inch-square leafing. This was allowed to tarnish down to a golden shade. It was then sealed to stop the oxidation from turning the silver black.

Lighting was kept simple. Central ceiling fixtures ran throughout with the same flame-shaped frosted glass inverted globes. The texture played off the screens. The illumination was softened as a result of a pale terra-cotta color that was used on the

(Above) ART REFERENCE: *Orange and Tan*, Mark Rothko (1954). The paintings of Mark Rothko, with their introspective, calming effect and similarities to the frescoes of Northern Italy and China, were used as inspiration for the plasterwork.

(Opposite) Crosscurrents of influences, European and Asian, are harmoniously joined. The Ushak carpet glows and the ceiling shimmers in the light of the fire; the bluestone mantel is disguised as an altar table.

ceilings. All in all, the colors throughout were reminiscent of frescoes you might see in Northern Italy or China.

Pale natural linen was the predominant fabric used. This helped to keep the atmosphere light. In place of sofas, a long banquette with cushions ran between support columns the entire width of the living room, like a window seat. Large upholstered screens behind the bed in the bedroom served as a floor-to-ceiling headboard, as well as concealing a newly created walk-in closet.

I am still amazed how casually the owner announced that she owned a collection of original Carlo Bugatti pieces. His characteristic furniture style incorporated inlays of exotic wood, copper, parchment, and mother-of-pearl. It was love at first sight for me seeing examples of his furniture on display at the Brooklyn Museum, and beyond exciting to unwrap tables, chairs, and a spectacular large screen to be used in the apartment. Carpets, Indian textiles, lacquered woods, porcelain, ceramics, and statuary did not distract from what was achieved with the new renovation. A gold-threaded Paul Poiret shawl even found a place thrown over the piano.

Although home to a boisterous little boy, other than the occasional skateboard going through the sliding door, a general appreciation and respect of the environment prevailed. It was through his later recommendation as an adult that I met one of my most loyal clients. More rituals followed over the years from that first purification ceremony. The sanctuary aided in the owner's quest for inner reflection and peace.

(Above) ART REFERENCE: *Paradise of Bhaisajyaguru*, Unknown Artist (14th century). Throughout the apartment pigments were applied to fresh plaster in lieu of painted walls, lending an atmosphere of serenity as in this Chinese fresco.

(Opposite) A nineteenth-century bronze figure and the Carlo Bugatti cabinet stood at attention in the entrance foyer. The pigmented plasterwork walls, with their striated horizons of tinted powder, seem to glow from within—a similar atmospheric attribute to the paintings of Mark Rothko.

(Above) The Japanese tansu cabinet holds a multitude of domestic items as well as media. The nineteenth-century Imari vase releases a shower of bittersweet and Chinese lanterns. Afternoon tea is served from a nineteenth-century English teapot. Very civilized, the table is set with items from various parts of the world.

(Opposite) The 1920s roundel is attributed to Hildreth Meière, famed for the Radio City Music Hall exterior medallions. Random bits of leafing enliven the frames of the shoji-style sliding screens used throughout the apartment to replace the former walls. Low levels of light come through the window panels made from wood and Plexiglas, backed with gathered gauze. Regency chairs appear to dance around the table on the Agra carpet.

(Opposite) The distinguished Ruskin ceramic pot, Paul Poiret shawl, Tiffany floor lamp and Carlo Bugatti furniture are all showstoppers, yet the total effect is still one of serenity. In the foyer, the single Bugatti screen is divided and mounted on the frescoed walls. The throne chair was made child-friendly with the addition of hand-painted cushions.

(Above) The linen upholstered wall panels serve as a headboard as well as for concealing storage. A glazed terra-cotta ceiling and the inverted flame fixture illuminate the bedroom. The opulence of the exotic quilt made from antique sari borders and mirrored Moroccan textiles for bedding was eased by the use of simple Japanese wood chests as night tables. The dressing mirror, a nineteenth-century gilt cheval glass from Spain, reflects the Ushak carpet.

Driving through the bucolic hamlet with rustic-looking residences, for a moment the Hudson River was visible through the trees and then it disappeared. As we pulled into the driveway, I saw a very large unattractive brown house and suddenly my heart sank. Stephen, my business partner at the time, explained that we would pick up a key and then look at the place to the right, next door. Relieved, we approached a white clapboard split-level house from the 1940s. When we got inside, it was very difficult to look past the existing dark wood everywhere and the sad furnishings.

A few days before, we visited the client's apartment in Manhattan to talk about working on the house and to see some of her possessions. Her apartment had been painted the brightest white I had ever seen and this was on every surface. She had a few homes. This one seemed to be more of an art gallery. There was very little furniture, but there was a large, striking collection of photography including black-and-white prints by Herb Ritts and stills in washed-out colors from obscure Hollywood films. The owner had taken some of the most beautiful photographs herself. The subject matter reminded me of movies where art by Salvador Dalí was sometimes commissioned—films like *Lady in the Dark* or *Spellbound* where the subconscious dreams that occur in deep states of sleep are evoked.

That visit was invaluable to get a sense of the client on many levels. Drastic measures were necessary to transform the murky rooms into a spacious, bright stage set—somewhere you could shoot a 1940s-type movie as seen through the eye of a Surrealist poet.

Like the client, the house had a few surprises to its character. From the front entrance one would never imagine that down the spiral stairs was a mammoth room with high ceilings in wood forming an A-frame with huge beams running across. On the south wall, the fireplace had a simple mantel attached to a flue that ran from floor to ceiling. Knowing that white would suit her, we still had some concern with painting over everything since it was all solid mahogany wood. We were given the go-ahead and before too long each and every room, including that mahogany living room, was gleaming white.

Sometimes trying something daring works, and other times it doesn't. When we were ready to strip and stain the floors from dark to light, the color of oxidized copper was suggested. The large room received the color first. As it went down, we agreed that it was "interesting," but when completed it was frightening. The room looked like the pool at the YMCA. As soon as it dried, the sander removed the copper-gone-green and translucent white went down throughout.

Undeterred by the floor-color incident, we still wanted something more exciting and offbeat in the entrance over the white floors. A black, blue, and white random checkerboard pattern was painted with stylized wood graining. This did the trick. It also gave us an excuse to get down and do some whimsical painting—a trademark design stamp which is always enjoyable. The wood grain technique was so effective that some of the beams surrounding the dining area and the fireplace flue were also done in this finish. It added to the fantastic hallucinatory effect with its pronounced undulating veins.

The term *surreal* has become a catchphrase for the odd, but we weren't looking for things with that quality alone. What we were looking for was offbeat, large-scale items, and luckily we had one Paul Frankl club chair to use as a starting point. We went to resources in a number of cities in search of chunky furniture to use as sculptural objects—as in a de Chirico landscape throwing off any consistent sense of scale.

While going through the storage warehouse in one of the more interesting shops in Manhattan, a half-sphere in brass with multiple arms was spotted on the top of tall industrial shelving. It looked like a porcupine that had been in an accident. The store owner said that it was just half of a complete sphere and that there was also a second one. They were light fixtures that had previously hung in a commercial space. The size was phenomenal and they would be pivotal in establishing the bigness we were after. An auto mechanic restored the dented domes of the chandelier, straightened the 140 spokes on each, and then sprayed them with a white car finish. Once they were hung from the high ceiling, it was deceiving that they were over four feet in circumference.

On one of the shopping trips that brought us to Philadelphia, the twin to the existing Frankl chair was found, then shortly after a sofa. Although tremendous, they also fooled you into thinking that the size was average until you sat in them. Two cork tables, also by designer Paul Frankl, were brought together from different states and painted white. The pair appeared like shoe soles.

To give the main room some detailing and to avoid hammering into the wood walls to hang art, a long continuous shelf was installed around the perimeter of the room. This was where some of the photography collection could be displayed as an ever-changing exhibit. Vintage Eames chairs, restored and ebonized, kept coming in like ants at a picnic—one more reminder of the Surrealists. Things continued with

(Above) ART REFERENCE: *Sun on the Easel*, Giorgio de Chirico (1972). Although Surrealism was the key motivation for the interior, long after the design project's completion, an uncanny resemblance was found in the de Chirico painting, aptly named *Sun on the Easel*. As in the painting, the interior-as-stage-set allowed the imagination to time travel.

(Opposite) Stars burst overhead from two metal chandeliers with points of light by the hundreds warming the walls and illuminating the ceiling and floors. Initially dark, layers of white paint conceal the mahogany wood of the large main room, allowing the furniture to stand out. The furniture by Paul Frankl is united while the Alvar Alto bent wood chair remains the black sheep.

petrified driftwood floor lamps, table lamps, and other unidentifiable creations like the organic formations in the paintings by Yves Tanguy. Running with this, a number of pieces of driftwood were brought back from the beach in Long Island and used as handles on the long low custom bedroom dressers. The wood was placed over the drawers and cut at each seam. There were countless innovative approaches and once the trust was established, we were off to the races and no stone was left unturned.

Similar to a movie, once the action took place it was time to strike the set. Unfortunately, the client moved on shortly after completion leaving me with uncertainty as to whether this all took place or had been a strange but fantastic dream.

(Opposite) From the moment the front door is opened, the picturesque hamlet out of doors is left behind. Asymmetrical squares of painted wood graining also appear as pools of water. The glass of the round window was replaced in blue representing planet Earth. The wood chair is a study designed by Frank Lloyd Wright.

(Above) Multiple sputnik light fixtures hang above the staircase while every other baluster on the balustrade is painted white or black leading the way to the dining area below.

(Top) ART REFERENCE: *Piazza d'Italia*, Giorgio de Chirico (1970). Assembling the art, the objects, and the furnishings in the house along the Palisades resulted in an environment reminiscent of a de Chirico landscape. The sense of scale and perspective questions the viewers eye.

(Bottom) The flue of the fireplace was painted with graining that can be thought of as wood, marble, moiré fabric, or white lines on a black surface. In the photograph, bison were frightened to leap over a cliff but are in suspended animation. Two big copper balls as firedogs were fabricated in the 1940s.

(Opposite) Biomorphism has connections to Surrealism, using slight characteristics to remind us of natural forms. In this room, an undulating figure as tall as a child with an equally high inverted shade appears as big as a table lamp next to the generously proportioned Frankl sofa. The two tables found miles apart nestle together as one. On the shelf that surrounds the perimeter of the room, ever-changing exhibits are displayed.

(Pages 104–105) From the sunken main room, hand-painted support beams frame the dining area. The top was added to the chunky twentieth-century vintage table. The insect-like vintage Eames chairs are ebonized. From the kitchen pass-through, a kidney-shaped counter juts out covered in linoleum from the 1940s. The black cast stone vase stands three feet high on the bleached wood floor. The flying saucer light fixture hovers beyond the sputnik in the foreground.

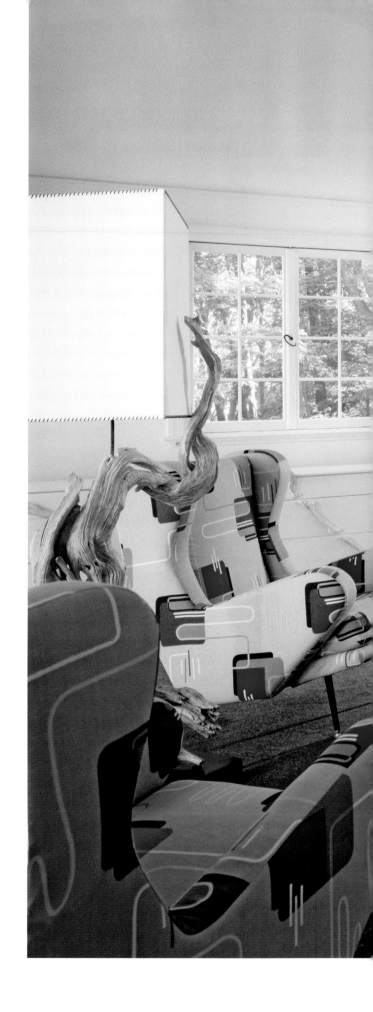

(Opposite Top) ART REFERENCE: *The Absent Lady*, Yves Tanguy (1942). The organic shapes rise up from the depths in the Yves Tanguy painting. Seldom there, the occupant of the house could also be referred to as "The Absent Lady," although her strong presence remained.

(Opposite Bottom) The glazier cut the kidney bean–shaped mirror for the powder room. Vintage linoleum was used to laminate the cabinet supporting a porcelain sink from the 1940s.

(Above) Playing off the twisted trees outside of the bedroom windows, the free-form driftwood lamps and handles of the credenza seem to move and sway. The Marco Zanuso armchairs are a sculptural version of a traditional wingback. For additional clothing, an upholstered wall was erected. It serves as a headboard and on the back side as a wardrobe. The stitching at its edges was hand-painted, bringing to mind a flattened baseball.

With so many interior design and appointment projects, the word *embellishment* is thrown around very often. This unusual townhouse in New York did receive more than its fair share of detailing. Ironically, the walls, floors, and ceilings received cues from a pared-down Arts and Crafts sensibility. Before my career partner at the time, Stephen Shadley, and I were commissioned to work with the owners, a number of major changes had already occurred—digging out a basement (a bucket at a time), removing walls in the stairwell, and adding a dining room with a disconcerting glass block floor. This was all in an attempt to open up the house and bring in more light. The work achieved its goal but sacrificed the townhouse's feeling of a home with defined rooms.

With the brutal work completed, the finishing details and furnishings would be addressed. On an early visit, a fumed-oak Stickley chair was sitting in the main room under a plastic drop cloth out of view. As we looked at photographs of pieces of furniture that the clients had recorded, we were taken aback. Precious antiques they had responded to, from different times and places while living and working in London, were recorded in the pictures. All of it had little to do with this house or the young vibrant American couple with a child and one on its way. Fortunately, the Mission chair was mentioned, and then revealed from under the plastic tarp. It was

unanimous that this was the best source for the overall design aesthetic as well as the furniture.

A cosmetic approach would not be enough. Trompe l'oeil eye tricks would not keep a rambunctious child from falling from the open staircase that ran up for three flights to the main rooms. With that in mind, we did a test using rolls of masking tape which we attached to the floor and ran up to the ceiling like prison bars, then went from side to side resulting in a large open grid. It was similar in feeling to the vertical square wood posts on the sides of our favorite chair, holding up the arms while allowing you to see through them. On each floor, ultimately an appropriately-scaled wood version of the tape mock-up was done to serve as handrails, unite the flights of stairs, and restore the sense of a central staircase without blocking the light.

Mother Nature would play a part, adding warmth and richness to the story. The few remaining walls were divided up in Mondrian-like sections with black square moldings in patterns reminiscent of the elements in a Japanese interior. These were sheathed in honey-colored wood veneer. Ebonized oak was used for the simple kitchen cabinets and the custom breakfront (a blown-up version of a Greene and Greene Mission cabinet). This was embellished with a back wall of ceramic tile that mimicked copper. Wavy Dutch glass was used in some of the doors. The floors in the narrow kitchen and the fireplace hearths incorporated Welsh quarry tiles that resembled exquisite mud. A skylight in the roof illuminated the glass block floor in part of the bedroom which, in turn, allowed the light to fall into the kitchen below.

When the house was gutted, a curved wall from an earlier renovation that concealed the kitchen was allowed to remain standing. Using it like a diorama that bulged out rather than curving in, a plaster fresco finish was applied by a Florentine artist and plasterer. Its stylized leaves and dabs of various shades of yellow ochre and burnt umber was three times removed from a watercolor pastel study that I did based on Vuillard's *Walking in the Vineyard*. The wall was polished smooth and waxed, and became a favorite of the clients' young son to touch from end to end while walking past it.

Natural light not only came from the roof of the bedroom, but the dining room ceiling and walls. Here metal edges supported the glass, forming grid upon grid. During the day, sunlight also made its way down to the basement level. The entire backside of the house had an industrial beauty similar to the iconic building La Maison de Verre, in France.

The facade of the house was virtually covered from top to bottom in wisteria vines, with a profusion of leaves most of the year. This was touched upon with the foliage in the frescoes. Bold, literal leaf patterns united the disparate elements as a continuous patterned carpet running from the front door to the top floor of the house. The carpet also incorporated the warm earthy colors prized by proponents of the Arts and Crafts and Prairie School movements, as well as nature lover and architect Frank Lloyd Wright.

The owner was very aware of the value of handmade artisan objects of all types. This gave us the freedom to custom design most of the furnishings apart from the

(Pages 110–111) An open grid, or simplified fretwork, in lacquered wood was devised to serve as a handrail and delineate the stairway where walls once stood. Three fumed-oak Stickley chairs were fabricated to accompany the one owned by the client. Copper was used throughout including the custom flat rod fitted with hand-carved rectangular curtain rings.

(Above) Leaves run riot in the curved frescoed wall based on the post-impressionistic return to specific details, so much so that the motif climaxes as a decorative border along the ceiling and into the adjacent powder room. A custom circular wood table with stretched leather top held by overscaled nailheads also serves as a footrest. The movement, shape, and coloring of the Fulper ceramic bowl add relief to the series of squares in view elsewhere.

(Opposite Top) Sacrificing a backyard, an addition in glass and metal opened up the townhouse. A basement was dug from the subterranean foundation. An asymmetrical wood-framed wall was added with various shades of violet in smooth stucco "Venetian plaster."

(Opposite Bottom) ART REFERENCE: *Woman Admiring Plum Blossoms at Night*, Suzuki, Harunobu (1765). The graphics in the Harunobu print and traditional Japanese interiors served as a guide for every aspect of the embellishments in the renovation. The Arts and Crafts movement owed a great deal to Japanese aesthetics.

Stickley standard pieces that were used. A more dramatic object was a hanging light fixture over the dining table. A combination of industrial metal and drab art glass made up the faceted circular piece complete with a natural linen skirt to soften the bulb's glare. Belgian linen was also used to upholster one of the walls in the dining room, giving additional texture and acoustic value. Movable fabric panels on the skylight helped ease reverberated sound and control light. In the living room, a leather-topped round table also served as footrest for the four Stickley chairs (three more were fabricated to match the original one).

Details became obsessive. The custom copper curtain rods were fitted with rectangular wooden rings, hand-carved to hold up the unbleached sheer linen. Belgian linen was utilized yet again for the free-flowing bedcover. Hand-embroidered oak leaves were strategically placed to appear random. This was thrown over a bed with a headboard that catered to the woman of the house. The iron that twists and twines with leaves and flowers added a touch of romance.

Adults and energetic children could live and play freely in the atmosphere of order and calm. With the balance of industrial and natural elements the house had attained substance, both in its function and form. All in all this was now truly a family home.

(Opposite) ART REFERENCE: *Chestnut Trees*, Edouard Vuillard (1894–1895). The muntins of a window frame the view and become as important as the chestnut tree and urban scene in this unusual (for Vuillard) painting.

(Above) The back section of the townhouse is a new addition. Mullions of the A-framed glass ceiling and the glass and metal outer wall are structural as well as visually dramatic. Light was the motivation for the addition and is allowed to work its way through the glass block floor down to the basement. The light fixture is a custom-designed piece in art glass, copper, and gathered linen skirt. The leather chairs are an early design by Mario Bellini.

(Opposite Top) A touch of femininity was added in the twists and turns of metal leaves in the headboard. It allows visibility of the wisteria vine through the glass balcony door.

(Opposite Bottom) Natural materials were manipulated to produce quarry tiles, wood paneling, and a custom-designed spin on a Greene and Greene cabinet. Light emanates from the kitchen's glass block ceiling—also a section of the master bedroom floor.

(Above) The addition of a fireplace and custom "his and her" wardrobes gave practicality as well as architectural interest to the master bedroom. To darken the room when necessary, a floor-to-ceiling linen curtain can be drawn in front of the skylight. The strip of floor was replaced in glass block to illuminate the kitchen below.

We met early in the penthouse apartment along Central Park West where the morning sun was strong enough to disintegrate the draperies, but the plants on the terrace and the trees outside thrived in it. My client had a modest-sized one-bedroom that I had worked on previously, and downstairs, slightly to the left, was a second apartment that he owned, but was using primarily for work-related storage. The idea was to break through and connect the two as one. Never hesitant to ask for help, I brought in Stephen Shadley. Together we found a good contractor, and after consulting with an engineer we were assured that we wouldn't have too much to worry about, other than the extensive permits required to proceed.

On to the design of what would eventually become a duplex. The top floor's long terrace would be accessible through large glass sliding doors from the living room and master bedroom, creating a wall of glass. This thought, and the desire for an indoor/outdoor continuity, was how the work of architect Richard Neutra came into the equation. Geometric, airy structures that blended art, landscape, practical comfort, and a touch of movie star glamour were his trademarks. To emulate this would be a tall order in the prewar, former Manhattan hotel—in fact, it was the antithesis of building a house in the desert. The starting point was to replace the wood floors with

slate, extending out and onto the terrace. A swimming pool, a typical feature of West Coast houses, would be substituted by Central Park.

Demolition started quite literally with a bang. In our plan, where the former galley kitchen was to be replaced by a generous staircase and landing to connect the two apartments, the cement floor took days to open, only to reveal a series of tremendous steel beams which we later learned were helping to support the water tower above. Our engineer's comment was, "I don't have a crystal ball." Ultimately, the load-bearing metal was redirected and we got our connection to the apartment below where we placed the new kitchen, dining room, and media room. The lower entry worked nicely as a service entrance for deliveries.

Another element that would invariably have been included in a house like those that we were referencing was a fireplace. With immediate access to the exterior, we were able to pull this off—quite an accomplishment in New York City. In place of a hearth, a long cantilevered shelf in slate was installed to run the entire length of one side of the room. A similar approach was taken at the base of the wall of glass doors, providing seating when entertaining a number of guests.

Although the ceiling of the upstairs apartment had been repaired numerous times, it inevitably leaked as a result of the open water tower above. Here a cosmetic solution that not only deterred the moisture, but also provided another element that coincided with the modernist vernacular, was to install a wood ceiling. This was made from waterproof plywood edged with a flat molding, then covered in a tinted varnish. The material was considered pedestrian, but ended up looking so refined—the reason being that it was one part of a unified composition and controlled space. This approach continued throughout the shell of the apartment, which incorporated horizontals and verticals using functional items such as the bookshelves, large wood and glass doors, the pattern of the slate tiles, and a boxy flue over the fireplace. All of this was seen as a De Stijl constructivist piece or a Piet Mondrian painting. Viewing the rooms in an abstract sense, we purposely restrained patterns to horizontals and verticals. This basic design allowed for excessive amounts of objects to be brought in while still retaining an underlying sense of order. What might have seemed restrictive ended up infinite in its complexity.

As in most renovations that are as extensive as this one was, time and money were key factors. Despite thorough drawings and plans, the scope of the work evolved both practically and aesthetically. The client never faltered in his determination to see it through, to trust us, and to believe the proverb that God, or the devil, is in the details—so much so that he camped out in the middle of construction for weeks at a time.

On the subject of details, while walking on Fifth Avenue, I spotted a service entrance door from the early 1940s. It wasn't exactly Neutra, but the design seemed like a way to add glamour to the pairs of doors that were being fabricated for the openings to the kitchen and media room. The exterior originals from Fifth Avenue were

(Above) ART REFERENCE: *Composition II with Black Lines*, Piet Mondrian (1930). The designs of Piet Mondrian, the most radical abstractionist of the twentieth century, were limited to horizontal and vertical lines, black and white, and primary hues. What may seem restrictive can be infinite in its complexity.

(Opposite) The verticals and horizontals in the three-dimensional space have a random order, while at the same time they are symmetrical and repetitious.

three glass squares stacked up vertically, each framed out and embellished with a brass stud in the center. Our version was made of limed oak, frosted glass, and faceted glass pyramids. Once installed, these functional but beautiful additions transformed the lower level markedly.

Finally, the time came to treat all of the surfaces. The remaining wood floors were ebonized black. The walls were painted in an off-white. Deep gray was used behind the bookshelves and the only shot of color was in the media room. Reflective surfaces would also be incorporated to give a lively play of light. Metallic paint and wallpaper were used to simulate metal—a material that is so much a part of modernism in art and architecture.

The furniture, as is so often the case in my work, included chairs, tables, and a sofa all in the style of the 1930s juxtaposed to items in the Neoclassic style. As time went on and personal objects began to appear, ethnic pieces from Africa, India, and Asia reflected the owner's multicultural background. I was partially responsible for the excess when I encouraged the purchase of a piece by a contemporary

Korean ceramicist. He became obsessed with the work and ultimately amassed a collection of over thirty pieces.

Although a stunning display, if the apartment was stripped of these fabulous objects, it would still stand proud on its own. We did achieve the airiness, the practical comfort, and the Hollywood glamour we were striving for. Even movie stars have made their way in a continuous stride across the living room slate floor onto the terrace to admire the landscape.

(Opposite) Plywood was used to cover the ceiling creating a grid. The slate floor consisting of squares and rectangles continues the infinite possibilities of geometric pattern combinations. The petite scale of the 1930s club chairs and sofa occupies less space, revealing more of the floor and a clear path to the terrace. In the theatrical painting Helen of Troy by A. Purwin (1940), the subject peers down from her place in Greek mythology.

(Opposite) The addition of a fireplace, a boxy flue, and a long, low, cantilevered shelf suggest the elements in a house by Richard Neutra. Silver wallpaper bounces light and adds a metallic surface to which a narrow black geometric pattern was affixed. In the background are five pieces by twentieth-century Korean ceramicist Bo Won.

(Above) A custom table in wood, leather, and silver leaf serves as a desk, buffet, and tablescape. A pair of chinchilla, or limed oak, finished lamps designed by James Mont form a relationship with the eclectic artwork.

(Above) The pair of walls that spatially define the dining room were painted to appear like rectangular sheets of steel. An actual steel base was forged for the dining table which is surrounded by French Art Deco chairs. The Empire chandelier is an entity unto itself, like an antique brooch on a modern garment. Behind the set of doors is the kitchen.

(Below) One of the few remaining vestiges of the original apartment was the floors which we ebonized. The opening to the left leads to the staircase that unifies the apartment's two floors. A second set of doors separates the dining room from the media room that also serves as a second bedroom and library.

(Opposite) Cutting through massive steel beams was necessary to install the staircase that redefined the two apartments as a duplex. One of the few curved objects, the steel handrail hugged the distressed painted walls.

(Opposite Top Left) ART REFERENCE: *Head No. 2*, Naum Gabo (1916). In the constructivist sculpture by Naum Gabo, mass was achieved through the use of open planes and the end result was substantial. These principles were applied to the architectural details as well as the structure of the utilitarian pieces (cantilevered shelves, freestanding bookcases, and privacy doors).

(Opposite Top Right) In the pair of custom doors, limed oak holds six squares of frosted glass and surrounds, and supports the faceted jewels in the center of each pane.

(Opposite Bottom) The angled plane of the underside of the staircase lends intimacy to the bed recess, which also serves as an extra-deep sofa. The bed base is also limed oak and contains storage for linens.

(Above) The high shelf was designed to have the buoyancy of an airplane wing. Five vertical wood support structures finished in limed oak hold the cantilevered bookshelves. Oxidizing copper was the inspiration for the painted ceiling.

(Above) Dark gray on a number of walls continues the constructivist approach, like sections of a rectilinear sculpture. The scale of the plywood grid was reduced for the ceiling above the main entrance. Through the simulated steel door, the master bedroom speaks a slightly different language than the rest of the apartment, but still holds to the same principles used throughout the shell of the apartment.

(Opposite Top) In place of a desert landscape, the typical surroundings of a Richard Neutra building, the urban panorama of Central Park and beyond is brought in to the interior.

(Opposite Bottom) Vintage grass cloth was used as a new skin covering the entire master bedroom (walls and ceiling). An ethnic mix reflects the multicultural background of the owner.

(Opposite) Glamorous photographs by Horst are hung randomly on the metallic walls. Different ceiling levels and support beams are accentuated, adding to the overall sculptural quality of the interior. Geographic study photo is by Sheila Metzner.

(Above) The view of Central Park and the east side of Manhattan can also be read as horizontal planes.

(Below) The slate floor of the terrace continues into the living room, or can be viewed as the living room plane jutting out onto the terrace.

GEORGIAN ORDER
Hopton Lane (Alfrick, United Kingdom) - 1996

Located in the English countryside, the Georgian house sits on the banks of a winding brook surrounded by high peak vistas overlooking valleys, villages, cathedrals, estates, farms, and expanses of woodland. The sky and cloud formations seem lower and backlit. Observing this, it's hard not to think of the British artist J.M.W. Turner.

A client that I had worked with on a number of other projects requested that I join him and his wife to see the estate, that he was in the process of purchasing. After passing through the gates to the stable courtyard, we were met by the former owner and her numerous Whippet dogs. She escorted on a tour through the house's many rooms, some of which retained the original Georgian style, and a few which had been added on in the nineteenth century. We proceeded to the cottage, stable block, coach house and the immediate grounds—all of it in great need of attention.

Despite the enormous amount of work ahead, my friends and clients agreed to become "Lord and Lady of the Manor." As melodramatic as it sounds, from the moment I was asked to be part of this undertaking, the feeling that my life was not in vain took hold. In time, demolition and restoration began and of course at every aspect of the work we were told "it's going to be a lot more than we figured."

The clients and I would have preferred to recapture as much of the Georgian period as possible. However, as a result of the house's listing status with the National Register and due to its age, any attempts to return the integrity of the Georgian period to areas changed during the nineteenth century were not allowed. In other words, we were stuck with the Victorian modifications in that part of the house. As with any design challenges, creative options replaced regrets. One such innovation was that instead of reducing the opening to the drawing room (as it was originally), we added a pair of wood columns at each side. They helped to narrow the space in between and were reinforced visually by the pillars at each side of the entrance portico.

The main staircase had been altered in the nineteenth century to appear grander. Appropriate to the eighteenth century, it originally had a single banister on the right and the wall to the left continued along with a door on center, resulting in a smaller opening to the anteroom. Staying with the later opulent approach, we left the double-banister staircase. A set of floor-to-ceiling gunmetal gray tailored curtains were installed where the walls should have been. This helped to shift the focus to the small room and beyond it, to the door at the farthest end in the dining room. Painted in the precise shade of gray, the pair of cast-iron Victorian support pillars (also a later addition) practically disappeared. There were numerous other instances that caused frustration throughout, resulting in something very nice although different than planned.

Getting closer to the finishing and furnishing stage, examples of fabrics, carpet wool, and color paint chips that were brought from New York were shown. The lady of the house immediately responded to a bone shade of paint unique in luminosity and depth. We later found that it could not be duplicated, as hard as the painter (or "decorator" as they're called in the U.K.) tried. We were determined to cover every wall, each door, and all of the trim throughout the house in this elusive shade. Even with all of the notable products there, the only option was to import the American brand. For a while, our painter became the resource for this paint in the region.

Although scheduled on a return flight to New York with prior commitments, the opportunity to paint the dining room with scenic murals was an offer that I couldn't put off. While I was shopping in London for metallic powders, translucent glazes, and other artist's materials, the room was being painted in a base coat of blue-green often used in the interiors of Robert Adam. Before removing my coat from the train ride back, the process of transforming the room to mimic the natural terrain began. On the south side, the brook was added, and a woodland grove of trees to the east. The hills and the garden fountain were the source of inspiration to the west, while the mantel received a wall of pines. Upon noticing a baby pheasant on the lawn, its portrait was incorporated into the painting.

Exterior workmen peered in to clock my progress. The light through the windows revealed a multitude of gold, bronze, and silver particles floating in the air and landing on every surface—myself included. Early one morning, the weather turned extremely cold resulting in a frost. I opened the window to greet one of the builders. Noticing the frozen dew covering the landscape, he said to me, "There's your metallic powder." Mother Nature was also doing "action painting." As the finishing touch to make it clear that the room's treatment was strictly decoration, a Greek key stencil was used as a border around the entire perimeter of the paintings. There was no change to my scheduled flight back home and the dining room was finished.

As in all homes, the work never truly comes to an end. The ongoing list has continued and natural disasters have impeded our progress but ultimately other things take precedence and it's on with the art of living.

(Above) ART REFERENCE: *Mortlake Terrace*, J.M.W. Turner (1827). Considered by some to be England's greatest painter, J.M.W. Turner inspired us to incorporate themes of light and nature into every aspect of the house.

(Opposite) Entry to the house is gained through the nineteenth-century addition instead of the original Georgian entrance. A pair of satin wood Sheraton side tables and two carved wooden urns used as lamps give symmetry while the asymmetric slate floor adds rhythm.

(*Above*) The portico is in golden Cotswold limestone. Numerous attempts to mimic a similar color with limewash on the rest of the house posed an ongoing challenge.

(*Opposite Top*) The settee and etchings, as well as the Classical motif toile curtain, speak to the Georgian period in this later addition. A ceramic garden stool supports a French Empire lamp.

(*Opposite Bottom*) The main staircase was altered in the nineteenth century with a second banister and wider set of bottom steps and risers. For compliance with the National Register, this addition had to remain. The Portuguese table is made from an exotic wood.

(Pages 136–137) In the foreground, a pair of mahogany fluted columns (found in a London antique shop), were installed to appear structural. The nineteenth-century cast-iron pillars provide real support. Beyond the drapery, in the former waiting area, callers could be seated. In the room are four Venetian chairs, a domed nineteenth-century wooden birdcage and a Watteau etching.

(Above) In the drawing room, the original marble Adam-style mantelpiece was paired with a Federal gilded mirror. Chinoiserie lacquered tall candlesticks were converted into floor lamps. The French Art Deco bronze pheasant strikes a pose on one of the Neoclassical marble and metal tables. When open, the cotton velvet draperies appear to be fluted pilasters. The wool carpet was woven to replicate the bone color walls.

(Above) The general mood and coloration in this room, inspired by the French painter Balthus, is continued and abstracted in the figurative painting by Teresa Pagowska, and then spills over onto the furnishings.

(Opposite Top) Visible from the southwest, a black-and-white timbered cottage with tiled roof is attached to the nineteenth-century annex and the primary Georgian house.

(Opposite Middle) ART REFERENCE: The Golden Days, Balthus (1944–46). This painting by Balthus encapsulates the sprit of the library and its occupants.

(Opposite Bottom) Black slate floors run through the powder/cloakroom and gilded-wallpapered water closet.

(Top) In the dining room, one of the windows was replaced with a door leading to the herbaceous border and Tudoresque herb garden. A contemporary table and Italian Modern chairs are at home in this eighteenth-century room.

(Bottom) Metallic powders and translucent paint keep the wall murals shrouded in mist. The pair of French 1920s marble consoles replaces traditional sideboards.

(Opposite Top Left) ART REFERENCE: *The Four Trees,* Claude Monet (1891). Japanese and Chinese influence is evident in the painting by Claude Monet. It served as the basis for my interpretation in the room's painted landscapes. The color choices for the furnishings came in part from Monet's famous garden at Giverny.

(Opposite Middle Left) Upon noticing a pheasant on the lawn, its portrait was incorporated into the painting.

(Opposite Top Right) The pair of French Robert Adam–style terra-cotta urns were found in Nice, France.

(Opposite Bottom Left) On an especially sunny day, western light illuminates the room.

(Opposite Bottom Right) A newly carved white marble Classical mantel was fabricated for the room. The Greek key stencil runs over and around all the painted walls. A Venetian Baroque mirror, Japanese vases, and a Rococo clock round out the period mix.

(Above) In the first-floor guest sitting room, the gray velvet and striped satin on the 1930s upholstered furniture plays off the painting by Teresa Pagowska. A bronze sculpture is featured between the set of windows. A pair of 1940s lacquer pedestal tables with mirrored tops (the second one is in the guest room) were acquired on a shopping spree.

(Opposite Top) Real and woven foliage engulfs the owners in Mother Nature. A French eighteenth-century tapestry serves as a backdrop in the master bedroom. An English Art Deco round table and plush armchairs add to the feeling of a hotel retreat.

(Opposite Middle) The first-floor staircase and landing repeat the pilaster effect of the curtains. A fabric runner helps to protect the Chippendale table from the southern exposure. An electrified bell-jar hanging fixture adds authenticity.

(Opposite Bottom) In order to fill the large guest room, a pair of beds with theatrical fabric canopy hangings was devised. In contrast, flat shades were used on the windows. The black-and-white photograph was taken by the owner.

(Opposite Top) A kitchen in France that the owners liked was the model for this renovation. The work surface doubles as a table for casual dining. As it would have in the eighteenth century, the stove remains lit indefinitely.

(Opposite Bottom) The black slate floor continues into the kitchen from the entrance foyer. Wallpaper with stylized flowers lines the backside of the open shelving unit.

(Above Left) The odd-sized limestone mantel was originally in a Sir Edwin Lutyens' building. A gilded Federal mirror was found in a local shop. The four Venetian painted chairs are nineteenth-century. In the foreground, a Herman Miller round metal and glass table keeps the room luminous.

(Above Right) To the north, the clock in the stable block keeps the hour. Replacing the horses, a portion of the stable is a game room that sometimes serves as a theater.

(Bottom) A pair of yew clipped to create one archway reveals a Victorian lead fountain that was found in a remote shop in London.

(Opposite Top) Looking west, the cottages, with their views of the property, provide a charming residence of their own.

(Opposite Bottom) The pool originally installed in the 1960s was briefly used as a lily pond. After a complete redo, it is now a "green" pool. Behind the pergola is the vegetable garden.

(Top) Rows of pines lead the way to the small bridge over the brook, dusted in snow.

(Bottom) A London art dealer found the watercolor of the property from the 1850s. Its coloring is reminiscent of the beloved Turner painting *Mortlake Terrace*—the first art inspiration.

Our goal was that everything should look as though it had always been this way—or at least have the quality of a movie set that was done in one era to look like another. All of this, although challenging, seemed second nature to me. Multiple viewings of such movie classics as *Young Bess*, *The Private Life of Henry VIII*, *Robin Hood*, and *Ivanhoe*, were the perfect references in my imagination for combining Technicolor, cinemascope and the occasional authentic touch. A few Tudor motifs were incorporated to help with visual continuity. Fronts of cabinet doors were given linen fold carvings, others were done in diamond-patterned leaded glass, and antique iron lighting fixtures were hung throughout. This all paid homage to Vermeer's paintings and the rooms that he meticulously detailed.

A good working relationship had already been established with the clients, having worked with them on an apartment in the infamous Dakota, where Gothic, Renaissance, and Victorian styles dominated. It wasn't Tudor, but it shared some of the qualities of the country house. In both dwellings, the overall idea was to give a sense of family history to the furnishings. This I interpret as eclecticism and was even pleased to hear guests comment, "Have you always had those sofas?" The major difference on this project was that we wanted the place to look as though it might have been done in the 1930s when the house was built.

Once all of the construction began to die down and we could actually walk through the butler's pantry into the kitchen, and through the newly created family room, we began to feel the satisfaction of breathing new life into these areas. We were almost tempted to go wild and paint all of the oak paneling in the drawing room a creamy white, (reminiscent of early work by the designer Elsie de Wolfe) but the owner wasn't having it. In fact, more richness and the sumptuousness of carpets and tapestries became the focus. We attempted to emulate Dutch and Spanish seventeenth-century paintings, where carpets were not only on the floors, but also draped over refractory tables, and where tapestries were often used in place of framed paintings.

Off we went on a quest to find these items in the proper scale for these oversized rooms. The largest carpet is in the drawing room and was actually from one of the palaces of the former shah of Iran. Even this huge piece left a considerable expanse of bare wood, but the central medallion—like a snowflake stained glass window—and the dominant red certainly did the trick to add the richness the owner desired.

It's always wonderful to get outdoors and touch upon the exterior of a project. Here, the same masterful blacksmith that produced beautiful curtain rods and cabinet details also made a custom hammered-iron garden gate to great effect. The seclusion initially sought was encroached upon over the course of time, which led to extensive planting at the borders of the property that included a number of fruit trees, pines, and various other substantial specimens. This added to the house as a private enclave.

Although families change, children grow, and interests lie elsewhere, this pile of stones waits amongst the trees for humans to add the spark of life once more.

Moving from place to place was a common occurrence for the owner of this Tudor Gothic Revival house. In fact, he had lived all over the world as a result of growing up in a military family. When deciding to relocate yet again from a residence along the Hudson River, privacy, safety, and little or no traffic were the basic prerequisites. He was shown a large house and grounds which would require a long walk to get from one end to the other. Set back on a higher elevation, the house looks like a nobleman's stronghold. He didn't realize he was looking for a castle. Built in the 1930s, the facade is in limestone, timber, and stucco, with leaded glass windows and a slate roof. The quality of the work showcased what builders could do in America at that time when given the opportunity. Its solidity struck a chord and it was there that he decided to put down roots.

The house became the family home. Time passed and decades later it was more than ready for renovation. This is when I arrived on the scene. In keeping with a modern trend, an entirely new kitchen was the first thing on our agenda. The rooms would all get fresh plaster and paint. Furnishings would all be replaced and the master bath would get designed and relocated.

(Above) ART REFERENCE: *The Artist's Studio*, Jan Vermeer (1665–1666). Vermeer is paid homage to in the 1930s Tudor and Gothic Revival residence. Tapestries, carpets, and the metal chandelier could have come straight from the seventeenth century.

(Opposite) A Persian Kirman carpet leads the way to the terrace. A large Flemish tapestry fragment is juxtaposed to the recurring pairs of 1930s club chairs.

(Opposite) Looking at the back of the house is made easier in the late fall. The chimneys, slate roof, limestone, and rock were artfully assembled by Depression-era craftsman.

(Above) One might expect Errol Flynn to descend the red carpeted staircase, as in the film *The Adventures of Robin Hood*.

(Pages 154–155) The vast drawing room works perfectly for recitals and other large gatherings. For this reason, it was purposely left sparsely furnished. Once covering the floor of a Middle Eastern palace, the Nain carpet motifs glorify nature, as does the plaster ceiling.

(Top) When the paisley wool curtains are drawn in the second-floor family room, movies that inspired the interiors may be watched.

(Middle) The Fine Tabriz hunting scene serves as art underfoot, while the menacing spiked iron chandelier looms overhead. The mica shades on the 1920s floor lamps glow when lit in the evening.

(Bottom) The breakfast room chairs are reminiscent of those designed by French architect Jean Prouvé. The original diamond pattern in the leaded glass windows was picked up throughout the many rooms of the house.

(Opposite Top Left) The vast majority of the chandelier and sconces were custom-made and installed when the house was built. A pair of French reverse-glass paintings from the 1920s depicts a Grecian couple with stylized cypress trees in the background.

(Opposite Top Right) The limestone fortification wall appears to be a turret from the bedroom terrace. It protects and gives a sense of safety.

(Opposite Middle Left) In the newly created butler's pantry off of the main dining room, cabinets repeat the original door arch leaded glass and linenfold pattern.

(Opposite Middle Right) A view of the terrace is framed through the Gothic-styled door. A grill in the countertop may be used during inclement weather.

(Opposite Bottom Left) Refreshments from this section of the kitchen make their way into the breakfast room and beyond. The diamond patterns in the glass doors were picked up from the original windows in parts of the house.

(Opposite Bottom Right) On one side of the vast main kitchen, the custom steel hood is reminiscent of armor.

(Opposite Top) Fine reproduction chairs and table in the style of Queen Anne, also from the 1920s, add a touch of fluidity and family heirloom eclecticism.

(Opposite Bottom) The 1960s art glass vase catches the eye on top of this Gothic cabinet—the source for the linenfold carving that was repeated on new cabinet doors in the kitchen.

(Above) In the library, a 1930s Italian tapestry appears to vibrate off the wall. Candlesticks, like the ones at Notre Dame Cathedral, were transformed into lamps for either side of the Art Deco sofa.

159

(Opposite Top) A print of *The Three Brothers Brown and Their Servant*, originally painted by Isaac Oliver (1617), hangs on the wall of the master bedroom—a reminder of the house's Tudor roots. More diamond patterns appear in the wool carpet and mirrored cabinet.

(Opposite Bottom) The goal of the newly created bathroom was to appear as though it was finished at the time of the rest of the house. The pattern of the windowpanes is repeated onto the upper half of the walls.

(Above) The walls of the master bedroom were treated to look like limestone blocks—castle-like, but more theater; sometimes referred to as "the glamorous dungeon." The vanity, as well as the porcelain lamps, are French Art Deco.

SCHÉHÉRAZADE SUITE
Chelsea (Manhattan) - 2002

A harem can be described as forbidden, protected, or sacred. This pretty much sums up how the owner regarded her ten rooms in Chelsea. As in a harem, many women arrived on a regular basis to perform various services in what might be the closest thing to haute couture we have left in Manhattan. I was brought in by a mutual friend when the environment was still a working one. During the apartment's first incarnation, I learned that part of the job requirement was to use your imagination. Stretching the mind became part and parcel of our working relationship.

Over time, the apartment became strictly residential, and then it doubled in size when the next-door apartment was purchased and we connected the two. In both phases, very large-scale pieces of inlay furniture from Syria (mother-of-pearl mirror frames, and an enormous armoire topped with elaborate pediments that looked like tiaras) dominated. There were also big dressers with deep drawers covered with patterns, leaves, and flowers set in walnut. Victorian and Art Nouveau sofas, settees, and chairs held up on casters of metal or wood in various heights popped up everywhere.

A taste of what was to make its way into the rest of the rooms had been done in the most private areas first. Bold and rich, the color turquoise covered the largest wall and was accentuated with silver leaf on the adjacent expanse. Dark, luminous, bronze-colored grass cloth on the support pillars between the numerous large windows added texture, looking more like silk shantung from a distance.

Set design, rather than interior design, was more like it. The vision of Leon Baskt, famous for the Ballets Russes costumes and backdrops,

can't be touched for sheer genius, but I would put my best foot forward. The approach had to be done with large broad strokes. I recalled when my Turkish assistant escorted me onto a plane, and then from one end of Istanbul to the other, spending days at each historic treasure. Experiencing Topkapi Palace firsthand was invaluable. The tiles, fabrics, carpets, grill, and metalwork—all the decorative arts in dizzying patterns exalting nature—that we saw used there would later be incorporated into the residence. Every attempt would be made to please the client who adored this type of opulence, and was by no means a minimalist.

The original open loft plan gave us an opportunity to separate the space with found architectural details. To enter the dressing room, powder room and bath, an elaborate former exterior iron gate was made to roll to one side. Old, extremely tall glass and wood fretwork with Arabesque patterned panels arrived in massive crates from the Middle East. These panels were used as stationary walls to create a lounging area; its purpose was to be a semiprivate room where guests could take the hookah water pipe, relax, or read on low, deep, yellow-green mohair cushions. The backdrop for these banquettes was inspired by elements in the famous *Odalisque With A Slave* painting by Ingres. Here, the embroidered paisley from an article of clothing was magnified and printed on canvas, then installed floor to ceiling and end to end on the twenty-foot-long wall, visually turning the thread into rope. Other architectural fragments were incorporated to give the open kitchen privacy for preparation of tea, drinks, or to allow caterers to appear magically with trays of hors d'oeuvres. The second kitchen was used primarily to prepare meals.

More comfortable long, low custom sofas were made, incorporating patterned embroidered back cushions in a chocolate plush mohair fabric. Another couch from the 1970s with a slightly eighteenth-century frame was redone in a deep rose pink.

Along with an extensive collection of vintage clothing and textiles, there was a cherished embroidered silk weaving which had been backed and framed to hang on the wall. With all of the windows, murals and most of the walls covered in top-to-bottom custom-designed cabinets to house the collections, we were running out of space. The solution to using this piece was to build a table in clear Plexiglas (we needed a large table in any event). This would incorporate the antique textile inside a translucent box and allow for an intimate inspection of the gold threads while dining on the protective top surface.

The use of gold is something taboo these days, often considered vulgar—although it's used to full effect in each and every period and culture throughout the globe. Staying true to the lavishness the client

(Above) ART REFERENCE: *Oriental Scenery Design*, Léon Samoilovitch Bakst (1910). A profound shift to overscaled, broad strokes came from the stage designs of Leon Bakst, particularly for *Schéhérazade*.

(Opposite) Architectural fragments from the Mediterranean Basin vie for attention with the magnified embroidery wall covering in the hookah lounge area. Silver footstools from India and ottomans from Lebanon provide low surfaces.

and I both favored, wood cabinet doors were covered in gold leaf, and then encased in Plexiglas. When the cabinet was assembled they all lined up in a grid to fill an entire recessed niche in the dining area. In certain lights, it appears like a blazing sunset.

The decoration and design process continued for a number of years. The constant embellishment was drawn from a wide range of sources including La Alhambra in Grenada, Reales Alcázares in Seville, and the Shah Mosque in Isfahan. These made their way in, but were manipulated on the office computer. After generating the artwork, it was turned into canvas panels, or wall coverings. The use of mathematics in the original tile work was now used to create these images to fit the spaces exactly. They were glued to the flat areas, between the ceiling beams.

Finally, we started to run out of things to cover in gold or other metallic light-reflecting and -refracting materials. The magpie love of shine and collecting was temporarily satisfied in this environment but there is more to the story. In addition, we were simultaneously working for the client on another flat in another country, as well as a flagship commercial showroom in Manhattan. These were decorated with the same obsessive attention to detail. Throughout all of these, the spirit of Bakst, the Ballets Russes, and Moorish architecture carried through.

(Above) The appeal of gold doesn't tarnish, nor does the thread in this embroidered textile, here encased in a large Plexiglas dining table. The doors of the cabinet are in gold leaf, also behind plastic, and in certain lights glow like the setting sun.

(Opposite) The ceiling's flat areas were covered in images of geometric repetitive patterns from Iran, Turkey, and Spain. The floors throughout are done in ebonized wood, as are the furniture frames. A wide variety of black industrial fabrics was used to upholster the Eastlake pieces, clearly visible through the dining table. Here, fretwork sections were used to enclose the kitchen.

(Page 166) Works by Diego Giacometti served as the prototype for this custom-designed and beautifully executed freestanding tree (one of a pair). It can be used to display pieces from the archive of garments and textiles, or as a sculpture.

(Page 167) A rose pink tufted couch in the study sits in front of a mural of a reclining woman, as in a harem. A collection of beaded handbags hangs like ripened fruit from the metal limb.

(Above Top Left) Square metal tubing was used to create the cages hung with movable panels of sheer embroidered linen. Here they are used as twin sleeping quarters complete with vintage, hand-embroidered bed coverlets.

(Above Bottom Left) A flea market find, the metal shelving brackets, were fitted with thick glass and display an exotic array of objects.

(Above Right) ART REFERENCE: *Costume design for Nijinsky in 'Le Festin,'* Leon Bakst (1909). In the Bakst illustration, Nijinsky strikes a pose repeated in the arabesques of the iron gate.

(Opposite) Beyond the movable Italian ironwork, silver walls surround a Syrian mother-of-pearl inlay dresser. A collection of art glass sits on top. The pale floors of Indian slate run throughout the dressing area, walk-in closet, and into the bath.

DIGITAL BEAUX ARTS
Carnegie Hill (Manhattan) - 2005

As I waited for my clients to arrive at the Carnegie Hill site where their new apartment was located, a disgruntled neighbor asked, "When is the work here going to end?" I was wondering the same thing and couldn't really answer the question. I had been told that their portion of the building would soon be "turnkey" ready, meaning once their furniture arrived they could move in. Despite all the activity, we did walk through the extraordinary space and tried to decipher where their apartment would start and where it would end. A number of questions were partially answered regarding the building, its history, exactly what was original, and what wasn't.

Extremely excited about being asked to be a part of something so unusual in Manhattan, once back at the office I looked at article after article about the once private home from 1918. The more I read, the more it seemed like the main building and the sister building directly next to it had a long history of continuous construction. Gathering the information would establish a direction, or at least reinforce what not to do. Plus, it's always intriguing to get the lowdown on former owners and occupants, who in this case, it seemed, were not blessed with longevity.

According to Michael Kathrens's definitive book *American Splendor*, the architect Horace Trumbauer, who designed a number of private buildings in Manhattan and many sprawling estates in Newport, was hired by a banker to design a classical

French house for this site. Evoking the Louis XVI period using the principles of Neoclassical architecture from the late eighteenth century, but with minimal use of ornamentation, the large but well-proportioned house isn't overwhelming.

Regarding the interior's early furnishings, it was the word at the time to import most everything from Europe in a consistent style to go with the architecture. More often empty than occupied, ultimately the building was sold and served as a school which remained until a developer purchased it and created a second building that together with the original make up five residences.

My clients acquired the apartment occupying the second and third floors. In the well-preserved entrance hall on the street level, the original winding marble staircase leads directly to the large, totally intact foyer. The living room, once the grand salon, seamlessly leads to the master suite, which is in the 2007 Palladio Award–winning new addition.

Any excuse to incorporate Neoclassicism into a design is good enough for me, but here there were many valid reasons to go that route. We wouldn't take any cues from the original owner with an across-the-board French style. Along with the apartment, my client purchased a number of the original crystal chandeliers that hung throughout. Despite the fact that he felt they should be included, we would only use them in the master bedroom and foyer. When I found four bronze chandeliers with Greek key motifs I knew that they would work nicely instead of the crystal, and establish a more masculine approach in the room. One of the clients agreed. I thought it was amusing that the man of the house wanted the crystal and the woman of the house preferred the bronze. She was extremely instrumental in so many of the opportunities to shift everything throughout the apartment in a more interesting direction.

As it happened, a friend of mine had attended the former school. I asked her to come back and try to recall how the interiors looked, particularly in the grand salon. From her recollection, all of the paneling that lined the walls and the double doors was glazed in a pale green. Details and moldings were gilded. This was interesting information, but the new owner was set on warm walnut for all of the wood boiserie. The traditional furnishings from various periods, the classical statuary and klismos-style chairs—all this would be turned upside down by a multicolored modernist carpet, a theatrical wall mural, and a number of custom contemporary pieces.

We didn't go to France for furniture, but that's where we drew many of our inspirations from. First, it was the paintings of Léger that would be reinterpreted for the design of the enormous carpet. Less industrialized and more romantic, the rug would also emphasize the direction of the light from the three windows with woven bands of luminous silk within the various colors and shapes.

Rather than spending countless hours at a drafting table, huge chunks of time were spent at the office in front of a computer screen where most of the designs were generated. With elevations to scale, the murals of the dining room walls were assembled, bringing together the gardens of Versailles and paintings by Sargent and Van Gogh within a framework based on eighteenth-century etchings of Roman wall paintings. All of this was essentially painted digitally, then printed on wide canvas to be installed floor to ceiling by our most trusted paperhangers. Once installed, three

(Above) ART REFERENCE: *The Engine (Le Moteur)*, Fernand Léger (1918). As described by Anthony F. Janson in *History of Art*, Léger's industrial landscapes are "buoyant with optimism and pleasurable excitement." The design elements and their combination can be called abstract. The carpet-as-art-piece incorporates industrial beauty which although in contrast, successfully blends with the traditional Beaux Arts paneled room.

(Opposite) In the otherwise deep brown paneled grand salon, the colors and geometric approach of the custom-designed carpet are reflected in the brilliant blue bordered ceiling, playing off one another—a device often used by architect Robert Adam. The bronze fire screen was forged specifically for the opening of the original oxblood marble mantel. While playing chess, family members sit on nineteenth-century Swedish klismos-style chairs similar to a prototype from ancient Greece.

weeks were required to cover every surface with translucent layers of paint, metallic powder, and a personal touch. Historically, using technological advances has been a means to an end for many of the artists that I most admire. The room would ultimately be the showstopper of the apartment and provide the vistas and gardens that were the only things lacking in the otherwise perfect (by the clients' standards) apartment.

Buildings that rose up over the years around the original 1918 structure allowed for a certain amount of natural light to penetrate, but left no real sense of privacy. In these areas, the glass of the French doors and lunettes were filled with Mondrian-like geometric-patterned leaded glass. Its shades of blue were intended to simulate sky and water, as well as the brushstrokes and colors of a Gustav Klimt (particularly in his earlier landscapes).

A few structural changes occurred within the apartment that caused construction to lag on. While this was finally coming to an end, and with the confidence that had been established, we were suggested to help with the furnishings in the main entrance and lobby. Upon the commission, we were able to have craftsmen in metal, marble, and numerous other art forms produce items authentic enough to have been part of the original supposed completion in 1918 (which actually would take nearly another century).

Life for my clients in the apartment and the neighborhood is not the formal gentrified existence that one would imagine. Teenagers racing through the rooms, social events, and family gatherings of all sorts keep a lively atmosphere that is reflected in the unpredictable approach that was taken here in the interior.

(Opposite) The Neoclassic hall is the most intact room from the original private 1918 house, complete with black-and-white marble floor and crystal chandelier. One door opens directly from the grand staircase, the second gives a bird's-eye balcony view of the lobby. The twentieth-century eight-panel woodcut-based print by Sam Glankoff (*Untitled*, 1978) continues the colorful abstract juxtaposition as seen elsewhere in the duplex. The artwork is flanked by a pair of tripod-based torchiere lamps, designed by Dorothy Draper for the Carlyle Hotel. The occupants toss their keys onto the Regency table upon entering.

(Pages 174–175) The three French doors with lunettes, although tall, still do not reach the eighteen-foot ceilings in the grand salon. From above, the four bronze chandeliers act like over-scaled jewelry to embellish and illuminate. Are the figures ascending or falling through space in the paintings by Belgian artist Caroline Chariot-Dayez? As in "Ode on a Grecian Urn," the room's focal point, a nineteenth-century vase, sits on a low marble pedestal.

(Pages 176–177) Shades of blue were used to suggest water and sky in the leaded glass French doors. As in a theater, the heavy curtain helps to absorb reverberated sound. A play on Roman wall paintings in the Third style incorporating a central image, here cypress trees and cascading fountains are framed with false architecture. The pair of cantilevered consoles morph out of the artwork. The dining table in the Regency style is engulfed in an Indian carpet depicting an aerial view of a geometric garden.

(Top) ART REFERENCE: *Schloss Kammer am Attersee II*, Gustav Klimt (1909). In the Klimt landscape, a carpet-like effect of countless evident regular strokes of paint was used, not unlike the pixelated effect of a computer image. Blues and greens are the predominant colors in this Vienna Secession painting. They are positioned next to each other as in a color wheel.

(Bottom) Blue and green continue to coexist in the breakfast room (off the kitchen), which is aimed at having an Austrian accent. The nineteenth-century bronze chandelier is the mate to the one in the dining room. Both were stripped of their crystals which were replaced by swags of chain.

(Opposite) The original white marble and bronze mantel appears freestanding in a lush park, composed to give a garden and views in the dining room. Venus is spotted among the trees, painted in a similar technique to one utilized by Klimt, but striving for the raw emotion of a Van Gogh.

(Above) The apartment has two studies, one for him and one for her. Here the lady of the house can enjoy privacy. The extreme ceiling height permitted a second floor, which serves as her fitness center with a cutout balcony allowing for the full span of the tall window. The "X" motif is repeated numerous times in chairbacks, footstools, fabrics, the desk, and in the metal woven grill of the custom cabinets. A contemporary version of a woven tapestry by Sonia Delaunay enlivens the room.

(Opposite) A second building was erected as a Neoclassical addition to the main structure. It works beautifully with the original Beaux Arts architecture, and there's a seamless flow to the master bedroom and children's rooms. A Baccarat crystal and gilded bronze chandelier was formerly in the mansion's music room. Subtle wallpaper imparts a painterly quality to the wall behind the headboard, where a computer-generated figurative image in a surreal dreamlike setting is placed asymmetrically.

(Opposite) The responsibility of furnishing the entrance lobby was turned over to me once the construction was through. Few changes were made to the original architecture but new alterations required a sympathetic touch. Marble pedestals were made to appear as though they may have always been there. Seasonal floral arrangements are featured in a similar approach to that of the Metropolitan Museum of Art (where nature is exalted and the viewer made to feel diminutive). As an acknowledgement of the building's French Beaux Arts period, a large Eugene Atget print of the park at Versailles was made and placed in a nineteenth-century frame. It is also a reminder of Central Park, which is within walking distance. The majority of the walls are done in faux limestone blocks.

(Above) The wrought iron gate not only serves as protection but also as an example of the high art of metal forging. On the front door, the lion door-knocker hearkens back to a time before intercoms. The newly fabricated marble pedestal is in a shape often seen on an ancient herm. Here the head has been replaced with a lead urn. Repeating this same shape, a wood podium was also made and serves as a check-in point beyond the doors for arriving guests.

The Upper East Side was the area a former client was looking to live in. Stepping onto a large terrace almost equal in size to the apartment, she finally made up her mind that this would be the place for her. Although we had lost touch, she called to say she was now ready, had wanted to work with me again, and was confident this would be the appropriate time. She was able to see straight through every obstacle that stood in the way of making this two bedroom open and airy, somewhat like a downtown loft.

I am always excited about the possibility of an interior design project that involves demolition and renovation. To begin with, there were tons of built-in cabinets to rip out, major walls to remove, a laundry room to relocate, and major terrace issues to deal with. The contractor, like so many others before him, used the expression "it's a piece of cake." When asked to do a job like this, the optimistic person usually gets the contract—and so he did. We started to draw, create schedules, get documents, and then hurry up and wait for the closing.

In the meanwhile we conceptualized the look of the interior, addressed the furnishings and fitting details, and inventoried the client's possessions. It has been my observation that the things that people are ready to discard can have a new life if handled well. There were many pieces of furniture from former dwellings, some that I found twenty years earlier during our first working collaboration. A storage bin contained a superlong 1970s sofa that didn't fit in the elevator of the last apart-

ment she lived in. All these items would have a proper place now, along with many new custom-designed pieces. The elevator in the new building wouldn't accommodate the lengthy sofa either. Too good to eliminate, not to mention years of storage investment, off it went to get chopped in half and reupholstered. It was to be the main object in the new lounging area.

Here is a hard-won lesson on my part regarding reusing things: retrofitting, or attempting to modify existing items—like doors with new handles, hinges, and locks—is almost always the kiss of death. The motivation to not be wasteful and adapt existing items, like good intentions, always paves a road straight to trouble. In other words, we have learned to start fresh whenever possible. The renovation went smoothly other than these few sticking points.

A good deal of the client's professional expertise is in color. Her basic preference and past experience of living with bright, true chroma would pose a problem in this environment. The job of discerning subtleties between one hue and another would be sabotaged by colored refracted light. Rather than painting everything stark white, my suggestion was to reference the paintings of Josef Albers and Giorgio Morandi, in which different tones of the same color were sometimes used. A long list of monochromatic neutral paint colors was selected. This gave the walls, ceilings, trim, and doors substance but lightness. We used the palest colored paints at the front of the main room to keep the entrance area bright, while the darkest colors were used at the window wall appearing further away and in shadow. Typical of my approach, the support and crossbeams were accentuated—this time using a subtle gloss to enliven them.

With my great love of plants, the client's desire to have them, and the opportunity to learn from a good nursery, the horticulture of the terrace started to take form. We wanted to have a chance to play, creating another large room open to the elements. Building restrictions regarding weight, size, and height (also no structures allowed such as pergolas, arbors, and freestanding trellises) temporarily stopped our plans in their tracks. The alternative was to use fewer sculptural large plants from the pine family that could withstand the wind, the freezing temperatures, and the hot summer sun. This we did to great effect. From the interior, the glass windows and doors appeared like panels in a Japanese screen. An onyx mosaic long table with a metal base in the form of tree trunks and roots added a touch of glamour.

Fast-forward to the Morandi exhibit at the Metropolitan Museum of Art shortly after the apartment was finished. The client e-mailed thrilled that all of her apartment's colors (which she now considered hers) were in his paintings. Aside from the palette, his sense of order and simplicity resulted in a very modern approach. From her understanding response, it was clear that we hit our mark on many levels with the project.

Through positive thoughts and a tremendous amount of hard work, movers were scheduled within an extraordinarily short amount of time for an assignment of this scope. Before we even realized it, an intimate group gathered to celebrate the completion with a catered affair.

(Above) ART REFERENCE: *Far in Far*, Josef Albers (1965). The work of Albers was the springboard for the paint-illusion of depth for the walls throughout the apartment.

(Opposite) This pair of square minimalist paintings, commissioned for a public arts project in the 1970s, was part of my early studio work. The concept for the apartment and terrace was to use furnishings as sculpture. The squares of the cowhide carpet in the lounge area bring to mind the *Steel-Magnesium Plain* piece by Carl Andre. Graceful and perfectly designed vintage chairs by Warren Platner are scattered throughout the main room.

(Opposite Top) Venetian Murano glass leaves were customized as wall sconces. Foliage from the terrace is silhouetted onto the wall through the sheer linen panels at the window.

(Opposite Middle) On the terrace, the metal trunk and root bases of the Italian onyx inlay tabletop were found at a local consignment shop.

(Opposite Bottom) A 1940s vignette includes a mirrored storage cabinet, lamp base, and two Matisse prints.

(Above) Walls were removed to create an open plan in the main area. Through the windows, sculpted pines of various types suggest a Japanese screen and also relate to the sculptural qualities of the furnishings.

(Page 188) A pair of Italian floral chandeliers was released from decades in storage. The client's request for wallpaper added a feminine touch to the neutral palette. *Study for the Great Divide* by British artist, Duggie Fields (1975) pops off the wall.

(Page 189 Top) One of a series of custom white lacquered cabinets was designed in my office, all featuring round relief medallions. Dominating square and rectangle patterns are softened by curved furnishings.

(Page 189 Bottom) By evening, custom sliding doors with one-way mirrors allow privacy while maintaining visibility from the client's private work area.

(Opposite) When the client is in New York, the apartment also serves as an office. It overlooks the terrace and grants even, natural light from the north. Custom vertical storage cabinets repeat the medallion motif and keep the room well organized. The kaleidoscope image of Kate Moss is by photographer Michael Thompson.

(Top Left) There is an uncanny resemblance between the French 1930s light fixture and the floral motif in metallic wallpaper in the powder room.

(Top Right) ART REFERENCE: *Natura Morta V. 853*, Giorgio Morandi (1953). Morandi's painting is spare and modern, yet softly romantic, and conveys the atmosphere we were seeking to attain—particularly in the bedroom.

(Bottom) The custom lacquered night tables with suspended drawers pay homage to Dutch designer, Gerrit Thomas Rietveld. Venetian glass sconces and the tufted cotton velvet headboard melt into the contemporary stylized wallpaper.

(Opposite) Playing up the structural elements is always part and parcel of our design repertoire, whether subtle or bold. The bed floats over a cloud of shearling. *Liberty* (1987), by British artist Duggie Fields, depicts Lady Liberty as a fashion icon.

My present interior design office and residence is in a designated landmark building that, in 1910, had the distinction of being the largest office structure in New York City. The southernmost tip of Manhattan is not really a neighborhood in the conventional sense, yet I share with others who live here a feeling of loyalty to the area after the Twin Towers were destroyed. For me, the decision to live on the harbor has been a good one and I now consider it my home. This time, the starting point for the interior design of the space was not only drawn from paintings, but also from photographs and movies of the film noir genre.

Photography's influence has been responsible for a major shift in my way of seeing the world. Its acceptance as art, in my mind, goes back to one of my first commissions in the early 1970s. While working for a client in a New York apartment, primarily painting the rooms as backgrounds for the extensive collection of furniture, folk art, and nineteenth-century American paintings, I learned of his admiration for photography. Casually one day I was shown a concealed world inside of his walk-in closet. The clothing was replaced with shelves, top to bottom. Here were stacks of photographs by Berenice Abbott, Brassaï, Walker Evans, Raoul Hausmann, Man Ray, and Dorothea Lange, as well as many other notables of Europe and America. To-

gether we edited them down to about sixty images that were then diversely framed using burled wood, silver leaf, lacquer, or pine according to the period of the work. My suggestion of hanging this portion of the collection in the same syncopated rhythm as the pattern in Mondrian's *Broadway Boogie Woogie* was approved with enthusiasm. Having worked intimately with the pictures—the printing quality, endless range of blacks, and the abrupt cropping—has stayed with me always. Thirty years on, while visiting the International Center of Photography, I noticed a sign indicating that my client had bequeathed his collection to the center.

In my office, as in the camera's eye, it's all about the light. Everything in this environment is either black, white, or gray. Some of the structural elements near the windows are painted ebony or deep gray, resulting in an effect similar to that of a backlit subject in a picture. A study in contrast, even the most severe sunlight is soaked up by many of the surfaces, including the black upholstered furniture, gray mirror tabletops, and black Plexiglas doors. The Carrara marble cabinet tops, white structural beams, and sheets of fax paper appear to leap forward. Geometric shapes wash over the carpet bringing to mind André Kertész and so many of the innovative photographers and 1940s cinematographers who were playing with abstraction.

The other major factor in the lack of true chroma has to do with the fantastic views: the ever-changing water, sky, cloud formations, and light on the architecture outside in a myriad of colors and tones. This would be impossible to compete with indoors. When working in natural light on design projects, reviewing fabric swatches, paint chips, carpet tufts, and reference material, the monochromatic room helps us to focus and make a clear choice.

After the move from a large loft with loads of stuff, paring down and eliminating felt very freeing. The possessions that would not be edited were the books. For these we designed a series of modular iron open bookcases to be fabricated by one of the last of the local metal workshops. Although somewhat impractical without a stepladder, the books run floor to ceiling, adding an architectural element as well as a reference library. Items that pertain to the function of the office as well as an archive of shelter magazines, public relations materials, DVDs, CDs, and vinyl records are all housed in labeled black boxes.

The view of the east side is primarily made up of buildings that range in style from Neoclassical and Beaux Arts to Modern glass towers. The multiplicity of windows in various shapes and sizes has a psychedelic effect, particularly when the sunlight is hitting them. Optical stimulation is played up with painted grids of rectangles in various neutral tones on the support beams, similar in idea to the paintings of Bridget Riley and Josef Albers.

Although a very generic renovation, the apartments in the building have high ceilings and odd-shaped structural beams and support columns, butting up against each other, looking like Dutch De Stijl configurations. These elements were emphasized and trompe l'oeil versions were done in paint where extra substance and tension was needed.

With the organization and order came an elegance and a serenity that is accentuated by the boats gliding along on the harbor water that appears to be at the same level as the windowsills. Figurative sculptures that once sat on every other surface in the past have been reduced in number. I now have the ultimate statue and world icon visible, Lady Liberty.

(Above) ART REFERENCE: *Danae and the Shower of Gold*, George Platt Lynes (1939). The deep black space is in soft contrast to the shades of white and gray in the photograph.

(Opposite) Reflective surfaces bounce light onto the mobile doubling its shower of discs. In the bronze mirror Parsons tabletop, a smoky version of the main room appears to be in another dimension. A mixture of old and new coexist, both inside and outside.

(Pages 196–197) Viewing the Statue of Liberty is a constant reminder of artistic freedom. Real and painted ceiling crossbeams and support columns appear stacked on the custom storage cabinets. Reference books require a stepladder on the floor-to-ceiling modular iron bookcases. Ebonized Louis Quinze–style chairs serve as desk chairs.

(Opposite Top) ART REFERENCE: *Movement in Squares*, Bridget Riley (1961). The flat painting defies sensory perceptions with its potent eye trick. Similar principles apply throughout the office in a less stark manner.

(Opposite Bottom) The thin black lines of the custom iron bookcases, Bertoia chair, and my minimalist painting are picked up yet again in the morning shadows.

(Above) In the main room, trompe l'oeil architectural details, painted and three-dimensional, add up to constructivism. The Hotchkiss mobile was hand-painted to coordinate with its shadows. Squares of light appear at random throughout the day.

(Above) The only unbroken wall serves as a personal gallery of work done for the space. The sculptural Empire Revival sofa from the 1960s is upholstered in fabrics originally intended for luggage. Photography reference books can be found on the custom shelving.

(Opposite Top) ART REFERENCE: Untitled, Duane Michals (1979). Severe lighting washes out my features in the 1979 portrait taken by art photographer Duane Michals.

(Opposite Middle) The bronze mirror-topped aluminum Parsons table from the 1960s throws the sunlight and patterns in opposite directions—subject matter suitable for photographer André Kertész.

(Opposite Bottom) The high-contrast detail appears to be black and white. A page in a book on George Platt Lynes is left open on the low silvered table.

(Top) ART REFERENCE: *Daily News Building*, Berenice Abbott (1935). In the black-and-white photograph, Berenice Abbott's work records the evolution of an ever-changing Manhattan. As the expression goes, "New York will be great when they finish it."

(Bottom) Four photographs by George Platt Lynes are lined up above the painted wardrobe doors. The reflections of cloud formations are uncannily similar to the painted doors. From this angle the shipyard in Brooklyn is in full view.

(Opposite) Floating above the bed are figurative paintings which were done as a practice using the materials and techniques of Caravaggio in chiaroscuro gradations of light and shade. A horsehair upholstered screen is slipped behind the custom cabinet for aesthetics as well as acoustics.

(Page 204 - Top) Roman statuary is silhouetted against the iridescent water of the harbor.

(Page 204 - Bottom) In the kitchen round bowls repeat the Clinton Castle structure's shape beyond. Another marble boomerang and ceramic urns continue the flowing curves.

(Page 205) In the front door entrance interior, *Reactor* by Kim Steele (1985) appears to be a detail from a 1930s futuristic movie, when in fact it is the inside of a nuclear reactor from the 1980s. In the foreground, a grid of Robert Adam engravings fill the entire wall. The wood tripod pedestal is Regency in style.

SAILING BELLE ÉPOQUE
Yacht (Italy) - 2008

When I was asked to join the owners aboard their sailing yacht that was heading to the South Pacific, I hesitated for a minute and then leapt at the chance. Months earlier we had worked together on a selection of artwork for the boat that consisted of framed photographs, mostly from the 1930s. They were now part of the boat's décor and appreciated by the owners as well as the guests and crew. Not too long after that, a new boat was commissioned. Its fabrication would take many months and fortunately I was asked to be part of the process, this time with a slightly more important role.

Naval architects collaborated on the steel-hulled 45-meter yacht, launched by an exclusive Italian shipyard. The innovations were new for the builders and designers, and the clients took a very active role. They were in on every phase of the sailing vessel's creation. When the in-house designers of the interior arrived in New York to discuss the direction that the décor would take, we had an extensive number of details to review. Although they generally handled all aspects of a project, my clients had a very specific concept in mind and wanted me to help convey it. This was where the nostalgia for the Belle Époque would come into play. There were a number of things to go over and many samples to be shown from our end. Just skimming the surface of an extensive list, we first dealt with the issues of color and style regarding the clothing for the crew, fabrics for many uses including window shades, cushions, custom bedding, interior and exterior furniture, carpets, hues of wood stain, and the list went on. Despite the language barrier, the response was quite positive considering how unusual our approach was.

My client was enamored with the detailing of the Cooper-Hewitt Museum on 91st Street, formerly Andrew Carnegie's private mansion. She felt that the most effective way to ensure that everyone was on the same page was to take a trip there. As we approached, our eyes were drawn up to the metal and glass canopy that resembles a parasol sheltering the entrance. With influences of Eastern Art (near, middle, and far), and the flawless combination of form and function, it has become an iconic symbol of the Art Nouveau period. These qualities were what we had envisioned for the sailing vessel.

Once indoors, it was the wood paneling with its numerous octagonal motifs that became the main reason for the visit. The eight-sided recurring theme, and how cleverly it was positioned in the mansion, would play out for the boat's walls, doors, light fixtures, and fittings. There would definitely be an old-world flavor. The challenge would be to integrate it into the cutting edge functionality and beauty of the modern nautical design.

My client had used the term *bohemian* repeatedly when she described what she imagined for the second layer of the story—regarding the furnishings, art, and accessories. I felt that I knew just what she meant but I've come to realize that no two people see things exactly the same. That's what makes it interesting. I had to smile to myself as I thought about the marginalized artists, writers, poets, and musicians during the Gilded Age, as we have come to identify it. This was an incentive to do something that might be considered bizarre or unusual. Hopefully, like the bohemians, our end product would be appreciated in the long run too. At the very least, I knew that an all-white interior with embroidered anchors on all the cushions was not how she wanted to express her individuality.

As the work progressed at a breakneck speed (for a project like this), questions came up on a regular basis. When out in the market gathering fabrics, that trip to the South Pacific and the work of Paul Gauguin kept coming to mind. His colors were over-the-top, some real and others from his imagination. Cotton velvet in brilliant yellow and a woven ikat fabric that was predominantly pink would go on two of the sofas in the main saloon. The third would not only be in a different shape, but be done in another fabric that was reminiscent of textiles found in North Africa. Purple was used on the fourth settee, and for the Roman shades, a woven linen in a green often seen in Moroccan pottery. Methodical lists were sent to the staff at the shipyard, complete with color swatch diagrams. Still, we received phone calls from Italy questioning, "Are you sure that the yellow and pink make up the same piece?"

A tribal carpet was found on a shopping excursion along with an entire line of fabrics that, although woven in Europe, mimicked the hand-loomed textiles of nomads. These were used throughout the cabins for the upholstery and bedding. The patterns were like those that Matisse included in so many of his portraits and still-life paintings. To me, he is the high priest of Bohemia.

In Chelsea, we made the rounds to some of the galleries with art for the walls in mind. We were instantly spellbound by a photograph of a rhinoceros that might have been taken in Sumatra and appeared to be the real thing. It was explained that the photographer had fashioned the mammal from clay and created the background. It would be our safari trophy, common among the elite from the turn-of-the-century, without harming the species.

We used other photography that had a 1960s psychedelic overtone. This was particularly obvious in the nude with sea grass projected over her sinewy body—the type of image that might be seen in the home of a rich hippie—framed in white gold, hanging under the staircase on the rich brown boiserie. Mindful of the instability of life

(Above) ART REFERENCE: *The Sacred Mountain*, Paul Gauguin (1892). Gauguin painted this image using one portion from the natural world and a large dose from his mind's eye. The color palette seems an unlikely choice to interpret as furnishings, but our sources are the same as that of Gauguin—nature and imagination.

(Opposite) In the lounging area, nomadic tribal textile motifs are juxtaposed to the Belle Époque era–inspired paneling and cabinetry. With a closer look, the geometric patterns can be found in each. The artwork, *Screw Auger Falls*, by Richard Wengenroth (2004) bears a resemblance to the sacred mountains seen through the window just beyond the grab rails. As fleeting as the views while sailing along, the artwork disappears to reveal a movie screen.

(Above) With a bit of old-world ambience in the saloon, spacious but intimate, family members and guests are made to feel at home. In the new-world cockpit, ultra-modern equipment utilizes the latest technology. The owners' suggestion of a flybridge forward above where the captain could control the yacht from a better vantage point resulted in more privacy below while watching a film or dining.

(Opposite Top) The main saloon comprises three areas. One dividing wall incorporates media, creates a backdrop for additional seating in the bar, and cushions the conversation area. Everything is united by the continuous glass parallelogram-shaped windows.

(Opposite Middle) A white gold–leafed frame surrounds the image Le Rhinoceros by Didier Massard (2004), known for recreating nature then photographing it. The points on the cushion's embroidery mimic the creature's horn. The plum fabric of the settee is also derived from the luscious coloring in the work of Gauguin.

(Opposite Bottom) A strap of cut velvet stabilizes the old-fashioned dining chairs. Natural light is allowed to wash over the teak floors. In the evening, the table is set with custom porcelain china and heavy crystal stemware evoking a time when it was customary to dress for dinner.

(Opposite Top) The octagonal motif is repeated in many of the yacht's fittings including handles, table bases, lights, wood paneling, and with a discerning eye can even be seen in the cut velvet upholstery.

(Opposite Middle) Toward the stern of the boat on the starboard side of the saloon, a freestanding mahogany staircase winds down to the lower deck and the four cabins.

(Opposite Bottom) At the bottom of the stairs, an evocative nude by Doron Hanoch was an intentionally bohemian choice for the primarily conservative boat interior. The double doors lead to a small lobby that accesses the owner's suite.

(Above) In the owners' suite, symmetry is used to heighten the elegance, including the illuminated octagonal recesses in the ceiling. The three blue-tinted early photographic studies of mammal skulls have been mistaken for embracing figures at first glance.

(Above) Black was used as a color for the bedding in the VIP cabin. The coverlet was fabricated from Moroccan-inspired woven linen made in Italy. The artwork, *Dolmen Balanced Monolith*, by Richard Wengenroth (2002), illustrates a massive stone appearing buoyant, not unlike this steel vessel floating on water.

(Opposite Top) ART REFERENCE: *Interior in Venetian Red*, Henri Matisse (1946). The Matisse painting includes not only the spirit of the furnishings, but also a North African vase in a sea of deep red.

(Opposite Bottom) The owner's bathroom is lined with Crema Valencia marble, continuing the warm colors with its orange and ochre veining.

(Above) Appearing the most like a vintage yacht, this starboard cabin continues the octagon paneling inlay pattern and a tongue-in-groove ceiling. Oil painted portraits of young Oriental women reinforce the nostalgic connotation. The beds can also be positioned as one.

(Opposite Top) At the end of the central corridor on the lower deck, the art by Nancy Burson (2002) is conceptual and requires a sharp eye to read its blurred message—"Focus on Peace."

(Opposite Middle) In the powder room, the inlay door, its handle, and the rest of the fittings all repeat the eight-sided pattern. Over the warm stone is an image of Venice taken at the turn of the century.

(Opposite Bottom) The banquette (with its exotic patterned upholstery) in the owners' cabin can be turned into an additional bed. Privacy is attained by deploying a movable partition. Voilà —another cabin!

on the ocean, large mineral clusters were displayed on the open shelves, securely attached at the base. These eye-catching formations were popular collectibles in Britain during the Victorian era, and we wanted them to be included in our modern interpretation of that bygone time.

First and foremost, the clients were extremely happy with the results of this collaborative effort. I've come to cherish our working relationship with its emphasis on the individual while still working as a team. The analogy is somewhat like the crew on a boat. I have since been included on a number of memorable voyages. One particularly exciting event was being part of a regatta in the Caribbean. It was thrilling to experience the true old maritime tradition, interesting interior aside. After days of being on a right angle, participants docked in the evenings and were invited to freely roam and view each other's prized possessions. We may not have won the race, but we received admiration from the nautical community regarding the boat's overall design. At the end of the day we were satisfied to be just where we were, although the next destination was in the corner of our minds.

(Opposite Top Left) While racing the yacht is equipped with a vivid graphic spinnaker to propel the boat forward.

(Opposite Bottom Left) An inviting corner is intentionally jostled by mismatched fabrics. The ever-present brilliant yellow attempts to capture the glow of the sun.

(Opposite Right) The sails rise almost 165 feet above the surface of the water. The 150-foot hull of the boat is painted in a deep red—a rebellious gesture considering the shipyard's tradition.

(Above) Boarding from the stern, guests gladly walk the teak plank, choosing to recline in the raised sunbathing areas, continue down to the cockpit, move on to the main saloon, or to head up the stairs to the flybridge.

ART REFERENCE CREDITS

PAGE 15 Gris, Juan (1887-1927). *Still Life with Newspaper,* 1916 (oil on canvas). The Phillips Collection, Washington, DC/ Photo © The Phillips Collection

PAGE 19 Vassos, John (1898-1985). Illustration from *Ultimo,* 1930. © Estate of John Vassos

PAGES 28–29 Moholy-Nagy, László (1895-1946). *K VII,* 1922 (oil on canvas). © Tate, London, 2010. © 2010 Artists Rights Society (ARS), New York / VG Bild-Kunst, Bonn

PAGE 30 Millias, Sir John Everett (1829-1896). *Ophelia,* c. 1851-1852 (w/c on paper). Private Collection/ Photo © Peter Nahum at The Leicester Galleries, London/ The Bridgeman Art Library

PAGE 33 De Lempicka, Tamara (1898-1980). *Portrait of the Duchess of Valmy,* 1924 (oil on canvas). © 2010 Artists Rights Society (ARS), New York / ADAGP, Paris

PAGE 40 Schinkel, Karl Friedrich (1781-1841), Loeillot, Wilhelm (1827-1876). *Perspective View of the Sea Terrace, Showing the Caryatid Portico and Glazed Semi-circular Side Bay,* 1847 (color lithograph on paper). National Galleries of Scotland

PAGE 44 Alma-Tadema, Sir Lawrence (1836-1912). *The Women of Amphissa,* 1887 (oil on canvas). Sterling & Francine /Clark Art Institute, Williamstown, USA/ The Bridgeman Art Library

PAGE 48 Watteau, Jean Antoine (1684-1721). *A Meeting in a Park,* 1712-1713 (oil on panel). Louvre, Paris, France/ Lauros / Giraudon/ The Bridgeman Art Library

PAGE 56 Sargent, John Singer (1856-1925). *The Libreria,* 1904 (oil on canvas). Private Collection

PAGE 63 Veronese, Paolo Caliari (1528-88). *Universal Harmony,* or *Divine Love,* detail from the ceiling of the Sala di Olimpo, c.1561 (fresco) by Maser, Treviso, Veneto, Italy/ The Bridgeman Art Library

PAGE 64 Lewis, John Frederick (1804-1876). *A Memlook Bay, Egypt,* 1868 (oil on panel). Private Collection

PAGE 66 Brangwyn, Frank (1867-1956). *A Trade on the Beach,* 1892 (oil on canvas). Musee d'Orsay, Paris, France. Photo: Photo © Réunion des Musées Nationaux / Art Resource, NY

PAGE 69 Gérôme, Jean-Léon (1824-1904). *Whirling Dervishes,* c.1895 (oil on canvas). Private Collection/ The Bridgeman Art Library

PAGE 70 Piranesi, Giovanni Battista (1720-1778). *Prima Parte: Title Page-State 1,* 1743 (etching, engraving, drypoint, and scratching). Smithsonian Institution Libraries, Cooper-Hewitt, National Design Museum

PAGE 76 Nevelson, Louise (1899-1988). *Dawn's Wedding Chapel I, from Dawn's Wedding Feast,* 1959 (painted wood). © 2010 Estate of Louise Nevelson / Artists Rights Society (ARS), New York

PAGE 80 *Frescoed wall of triclinium 'C' with two landscapes,* from Villa della Farnesina, Rome. Commissioned by Agrippa (ca. 25-20 BCE). Roman, early 3rd style. Photo: Luciano Romano Grafiluce. Photo Credit : Scala / Art Resource, NY. Museo Nazionale Romano (Palazzo Massimo alle Terme), Rome, Italy

PAGE 88 Caravaggio (Michelangelo Merisi da) (1573-1610). *Basket of Fruit,* c. 1600-1601. Photo Credit : Scala / Art Resource, NY. Biblioteca Ambrosiana, Milan, Italy

PAGE 90 Rothko, Mark (1903-1970). *Orange and Tan,* 1954 (oil on canvas). National Gallery of Art, Washington, DC. © 1998 Kate Rothko Prizel & Christopher Rothko / Artists Rights Society (ARS), New York

PAGE 92 *Paradise of Bhaisajyaguru,* mural from Main Hall, Guangsheng Lower Monastery, Shanxi. Yuan dynasty (after 1309, before 1319). Paint on plaster. The Metropolitan Museum of Art, New York, NY, U.S.A.

PAGE 98 De Chirico, Giorgio (1888-1978). *Piazza d'Italia,* 1970 (oil on canvas). Art Gallery of Ontario, Toronto, Canada/ Gift of Sam and Ayala Zacks, 1970/ The Bridgeman Art Library; © 2010 Artists Rights Society (ARS), New York / SIAE, Rome

PAGE 102 De Chirico, Giorgio (1888-1978). *Sun on the Easel,* 1972 (oil on canvas). Private Collection; © 2010 Artists Rights Society (ARS), New York / SIAE, Rome

PAGE 106 Tanguy, Yves (1900-1955). *The Absent Lady,* 1942 (oil on canvas) © 2010 Estate of Yves Tanguy / Artists Rights Society (ARS), New York

PAGE 108 Vuillard, Edouard (1868-1940). *Walking in the Vineyard,* c.1897-1899 (oil on canvas) 102 1/2 x 98 in. (260.35 x 248.92 cm). Gift of Hans de Schulthess (59.75). Digital Image © 2009 Museum Associates / LACMA / Art Resource, NY; Los Angeles County Museum of Art, Los Angeles, U.S.A.

PAGE 113 Harunobu, Suzuki (1705-1772). *Woman Admiring Plum Blossoms at Night.* Edo period (1615-1868). Polychrome woodblock print with embossing (karazuri); ink and color on paper, medium-size print (chu-ban). Fletcher Fund, 1929. Image copyright © The Metropolitan Museum of Art / Art Resource, NY; The Metropolitan Museum of Art, New York, NY, U.S.A.

PAGE 114 Vuillard, Edouard (1868-1940). *Chestnut Trees,* 1894/95 (distemper on cardboard, mounted on canvas). Private Collection

PAGE 118 Mondrian, Piet (1872-1944). *Composition II with Black Lines,* 1930 (oil on canvas). © 2010 Mondrian/Holtzman Trust c/o HCR International Virginia; Collection Van Abbemuseum, Eindhoven, The Netherlands; Photographer: Peter Cox, Eindhoven, The Netherlands

PAGE 126 Gabo, Naum (1890-1977). *Constructed Head No. 2,* 1916. Tate Gallery, London; © 2010 Nina Williams

PAGE 132 Turner, Joseph William Mallord (1775-1851). *Mortlake Terrace,* 1827 (oil on canvas). Andrew W. Mellon Collection, Image Courtesy National Gallery of Art, Washington, DC

PAGE 141 Klossowski de Rola, Balthasar (Balthus) (1908-2001). *The Golden Years,* 1944-46 (oil on canvas) Hirshhorn Museum, Washington D.C., USA/ Lauros / Giraudon/ The Bridgeman Art Library; © 2010 Artists Rights Society (ARS), New York / ADAGP, Paris

PAGE 143 Monet, Claude (1840-1926). *The Four Trees.* 1891 (oil on canvas). H. O. Havemeyer Collection, Bequest of Mrs. H. O. Havemeyer, 1929 (29.100.110). Image copyright © The Metropolitan Museum of Art / Art Resource, NY. The Metropolitan Museum of Art, New York, NY, U.S.A.

PAGE 150 Vermeer, Jan (1632-1675). *The Artist's Studio,* c.1665-66 (oil on canvas) Kunsthistorisches Museum, Vienna, Austria/ The Bridgeman Art Library

PAGE 162 Bakst, Léon Samoilovitch (1866-1924). *Oriental Scenery Design,* 1910 (colour litho) Private Collection/ The Stapleton Collection/ The Bridgeman Art Library

PAGE 168 Bakst, Léon Samoilovitch (1866-1924). *Costume design for Nijinsky in 'Le Festin',* 1909. Private Collection/ © The Fine Art Society, London, UK/ The Bridgeman Art Library

PAGE 170 Léger, Fernand (1881-1955). The Engine *(Le Moteur),* 1918 (oil on canvas) © 2010 Artists Rights Society (ARS), New York / ADAGP, Paris; Private Collection/ Photo © Christie's Images/ The Bridgeman Art Library

PAGE 178 Klimt, Gustav (1862-1918). *Schloss Kammer am Attersee II,* c.1909 (oil on canvas). Private Collection/ The Bridgeman Art Library

PAGE 184 Albers, Josef (1888-1976). *Study for Homage to the Square, Far in Far,* 1965 (oil on masonite) 24 x 24". 1976.1.573. © 2010 The Josef and Anni Albers Foundation / Artists Rights Society (ARS), New York. Photo: Tim Nighswander. Photo Credit: Albers Foundation/Art Resource, NY. The Josef and Anni Albers Foundation, Bethany, CT, U.S.A

PAGE 192 Morandi, Giorgio (1890-1964). *Still Life,* 1953 (oil on canvas) 35,5 x 45,5 cm. Inv. 598 A.F. n. 83. © 2010 Artists Rights Society (ARS), New York / SIAE, Rome. Photo Credit : Scala/Ministero per i Beni e le Attività culturali / Art Resource, NY. Fondazione Magnani Rocca, Corte di Mamiano, Italy

PAGE 194 Platt Lynes, George (1907-1955). *Danae and the Shower of Gold,* 1939 (black and white photograph) © Estate of George Platt Lynes

PAGE 198 Riley, Bridget (1931). *Movement in Squares,* 1961 (tempera on hardboard) © 2010 Bridget Riley. All rights reserved. Courtesy Karsten Schubert, London. Arts Council Collection, Hayward Gallery, London

PAGE 202 Abbott, Berenice (1898-1991). *Daily News Building, New York,* 1935 (black and white photograph) © Commerce Graphics

PAGE 206 Gauguin, Paul (1848-1903). *The Sacred Mountain (Parahi Te Marae),* 1892. Oil on canvas, 26 x 35 in (66 x 88.9 cm). Gift of Mr. and Mrs. Rodolphe Meyer de Schauensee, 1980. The Philadelphia Museum of Art / Art Resource, NY, Philadelphia Museum of Art, Philadelphia, Pennsylvania, U.S.A.

PAGE 213 Matisse, Henri (1869-1954). *Interior in Venetian Red,* 1946 (oil on canvas) 92 x 65 cm.; Scala / Art Resource, NY. Musees Royaux des Beaux-Arts, Brussels, Belgium. © 2010 Succession H. Matisse / Artists Rights Society (ARS), New York

PHOTO CREDITS

(Page 4) PROJECT 2007: A cast stone female torso is exalted on a black marble pedestal in the entrance. The Verrazano-Narrows Bridge sits on the horizon line out in New York Harbor.

(Pages 5–6) PROJECT 1975: The mantel and wall paneling are original to the New York private home designed by Horace Trumbauer, although the boiserie was altered in finish and composition. A custom overscale bronze firescreen was added for function as well as drama.

(Page 11) PROJECT 2005: A fleeting moment is captured in the ever-changing natural light flooded office and residence overlooking the harbor in New York.

(Pages 12–13) PROJECT 2007: The upward thrust of the architectural wood column dominates the corner of the romantically painted bedroom.

(Page 219) PROJECT 1980: The 1930s tuxedo shop neon figure presides over the client's diverse collection of cherished artworks. Paintings from the Ashcan School line the room. A charcoal cityscape and a Georges Braque drawing are united by the modeled background and the faux bois wainscoting.

(Page 220–221) PROJECT 1975: A sculptural element was the result of severing the surface of the wall, as in a painting by Cézanne.

(Page 222–223) PROJECT 2005: Fountains gush in suspended animation in the custom dining room wall murals. In the breakfast room beyond, Mondrian squares and rectangles of glass suggest water and sky.

First published in the United States of America in 2011 by
RIZZOLI INTERNATIONAL PUBLICATIONS, INC.
300 Park Avenue South
New York, NY 10010
www.rizzoliusa.com

ISBN-13: 978-0-8478-3592-8
Library of Congress Control Number: 2010931530

© 2011 Richard Gillette
© 2011 Rizzoli International Publications, Inc.
Introduction by Wendy Moonan © 2011
All chapters edited by Erika Mehiel

All rights reserved. No part of this publication may be reproduced,
stored in a retrieval system, or transmitted in any form or by any
means, electronic, mechanical, photocopying, recording, or otherwise, without prior consent of the publisher.

Distributed to the U.S. trade by Random House, New York
Designed by Richard Gillette Designs
Printed and Bound in China
2011 2012 2013 2014 2015/ 10 9 8 7 6 5 4 3 2 1